the
pow
of praise

sally jeffree

© Sally Jeffree

Freedom Publishing
12 Dukes Court, Bognor Road
Chichester   PO19 8FX
www.freedompublishing.net

ISBN: 978-1-908154-50-7

British Library Cataloguing in Publication Data. A catalogue record for this book is available from the British Library

Cover design: Esther Kotecha
Layout by Freedom Publishing
Printed in the UK

Table of Contents

Introduction.................................. 7
Day 1 – We are free to choose 13
Day 2 – Living Abundantly 15
Day 3 – Jesus is Lord 17
Day 4 - Every Knee Shall Bow 19
Day 5 – God Choses the Weak 21
Day 6 – God's Unconditional Love 23
Day 7 – God's Extravagant Love 25
Day 8 – God's Treasured Possession 27
Day 9 – God Will Carry Us 29
Day 10 – Inside Earthen Vessels 31
Day 11 – More than Conquerors 33
Day 12 – Nothing is Impossible 35
Day 13 – Plans to Prosper Us 37
Day 14 – Under His Wings 39
Day 15 – A Robe of Righteousness 41
Day 16 – Christ Sets Us Free 43
Day 17 – Jesus Will Help Us 45
Day 18 – Living Triumphantly 47
Day 19 – We Have Been Chosen 49
Day 20 – Seated with Christ 51
Day 21 – In the Heavenly Realms 53
Day 22 – Power from On High 55
Day 23 – Even Greater Things 57
Day 24 – Every Blessing 59
Day 25 – Please Open our Eyes 61
Day 26 – The Lord is My Shepherd 63
Day 27 – For the Joy 65

Day 28 – Sharing His Glory 67

Day 29 – A Little Can be Enough 69

Day 30 – I Will Give Your Rest 71

Day 31 – My Burden is Light 73

Day 32 – A Double Portion 75

Day 33 – Never Failing Compassion 77

Day 34 – Guaranteed Inheritance 79

Day 35 – Bond of Love 81

Day 36 – God's Word Holds Us Up 83

Day 37 – The Lord's Glory 85

Day 38 – Holy and Blameless 87

Day 39 – The Divine Exchange 89

Day 40 – Partakers 91

Day 41 – No Condemnation 93

Day 42 – Incomparable Riches 95

Day 43 – Good News 97

Day 44 – Alive in Christ 99

Day 45 – God Commands a Blessing 101

Day 46 – Kept from Stumbling 103

Day 47 – All Things! 105

Day 48 – Everything we Need 107

Day 49 – His Great Love 109

Day 50 – The Oil of Joy 111

Day 51 – Oaks of Righteousness 113

Day 52 – Predestined for Adoption 115

Day 53 – Predestined for His Glory 117

Day 54 – God's Workmanship 119

Day 55 – Unforgettable 121

Day 56 – The Lord will Take me up 123

Day 57 – Abide in Love 125

Day 58 – I Can Do All Things 127

Day 59 – Greater is He 129

Day 60 – Focus on What is Good   131
Day 61 – We Reap what we Sow   133
Day 62 – Guarded by Peace   135
Day 63 – A Way Back   137
Day 64 – If My People!   139
Day 65 – O Valiant Warrior   141
Day 66 – I Searched for a Man   143
Day 67 – For the Poor in Spirit   145
Day 68 – Come to Me!   147
Day 69 – The Battle is not Ours   149
Day 70 – The Way Up is Down   151
Day 71 – What is Love?   153
Day 72 – Lovingkindness   155
Day 73 – Drawing Closer to God   157
Day 74 – Rooted and Grounded   159
Day 75 – Filled with God   161
Day 76 – The Fruit of the Spirit   163
Day 77 – The Glory of Jesus   165
Day 78 – Mine is Yours   167
Day 79 – Rich in Mercy   169
Day 80 – Do We Have a Vision   171
Day 81 – Walk in Love   173
Day 82 – No Spot or Wrinkle   175
Day 83 – Buried with Him   177
Day 84 – God is in Your Midst   179
Day 85 – Quiet in His Love   181
Day 86 – Riches of Grace   183
Day 87 – He First Loved Us   185
Day 88 – I Have Been Crucified   187
Day 89 – No Longer Slaves to Sin   189
Day 90 – The Lord Stood With Me   191
Day 91 – Learning to be Content   193
Day 92 – When Less is More   195

Day 93 – New Every Morning 197
Day 94 – Channels of God's Love 199
Day 95 – A Pathway to Joy 201
Day 96 – Grasshoppers! 203
Day 97 – God is Good 205
Day 98 – We Can be Against Us? 207
Day 99 – Fewest of All Peoples 209
Day 100 – The Supremacy of Love 211

Introduction

Towards the end of 2019, before any of us could have imagined how our lives would be uprooted and changed the following year by the world-wide Covid 19 pandemic, God spoke clearly to me and said that we were about to go through a very difficult time and He was asking me to write a series of devotions that would help us, as Christian believers, to stay positive and full of faith during this time. I could not have imagined how close this time of testing would be.

I responded almost immediately and started to write this series of devotions which would focus on two wonderful and life-changing truths: the amazing position to which God has lifted us in Christ, and how very much we are loved and treasured by Him. I have learned over forty plus years as a Christian that the key to living victoriously is knowing how much we are loved by God and continuing to trust and to praise Him regardless of our circumstances, whether good or bad. Focusing daily on these truths should help us to do this.

I confess that, although I continued to write these devotions, I temporarily forgot the exact words which God had spoken to me and He needed to remind me in April 2020 that now was the time to share these studies. I therefore started to upload them onto our charity website prior to getting them published and made available more widely.

There are many Bible passages which exhort us to praise God especially when we are passing through times of testing and hardship, two of which are quoted below. In the natural, it is difficult and seeming unreasonable for us to remain thankful when circumstances are contrary to our comfort and security. However, this is the key to maintaining our emotional health and to seeing a difficult situation turned around for good.

> *Though the fig tree should not blossom and there be no fruit on the vines, Though the yield of the olive should fail and the fields produce no food, Though the flock should be cut off from the fold And there be no cattle in the stalls, yet I will exult in the LORD, I will rejoice in the God of my salvation.* Habakkuk 3:17-18

> *Rejoice in the Lord always; again I will say, rejoice! Let your gentle spirit be known to all men. The Lord is near. Be anxious for nothing, but in everything by prayer and supplication with thanksgiving let your requests be made known to God. And the peace of God, which surpasses all comprehension, will guard your hearts and your minds in Christ Jesus.* Philippians 4:4-7

I would like to consider two biblical stories, both well-known, which demonstrate the power of praise and worship. One from the Old Testament and the second from the New. We find the first in 2 Chronicles 20. Judah was being attacked by the Moabites, the Ammonites and the Meunites when Jehoshaphat was on the throne. Upon hearing that this vast multitude was coming against them, Jehoshaphat focused his attention on seeking God and proclaimed a fast throughout the whole of Judah. The people therefore met together, and King Jehoshaphat cried out to God in a prayer which is recorded in detail and well worth studying because of the many powerful principles included in it.

After his prayer the Spirit of God came upon Jahaziel who gave an amazing word of prophecy in which God gave very clear guidance to the people and promised to give them victory. God also told them that they would not need to fight this battle, for the battle was not theirs but His! What is significant in this passage is that the people took God's word seriously and obeyed it precisely. They believed God when He told them that they would not need to fight and so they appointed those who sang to the Lord to go ahead of the army, and when they worshipped Him, God set ambushes and the enemy was defeated!

The second story about praise and worship in adverse circumstances is found in the Acts 16. Following Paul and Silas delivering Lydia from a spirit of divination, the crowd rose up against them, they were beaten with rods and thrown into an inner prison with their feet fastened in stocks. However, instead of bemoaning their situation, Paul and Silas prayed and sang hymns of praise to God. As they did so, a great earthquake shook the foundations of the prison, all the doors were opened, all the prisoners' chains were unfastened, and the jailer asked how he could be saved. What further proof do we need of the power of praise?

Let us also reflect on the story of the feeding of the five thousand from a praise perspective. The disciples looked at this small but very sacrificial gift and dismissed it as being insufficient, but Jesus thanked God for what they had and when the disciples distributed it to the vast crowd, it was more than enough. This story teaches us that when we face insufficiency of any kind – it could be finances, possessions or even physical health and emotional energy, instead of moaning and complaining about our insufficiency, we should thank God for the little that we do have and even give some away to others. The way in which we can apply this lesson to finances is obvious. However, we can also apply it to physical health and energy: instead of focusing on our pain or lack of energy, we should thank God for all the abilities that we do have and seek to do some act of kindness – however small – for others instead of looking to others to care for us. Scripture assures us that when we do so, our insufficiency will be more than enough for our needs.

We have seen how praise and worship can release God's power in Malawi. At the beginning of 2017, the Lower Shire was attacked by the Fall Army Worm and communities lost 70% of their crops. The African

Army Worm is a known pest in Africa, but it dies out naturally during the colder season. This Fall Army Worm, however, was thought to have come from American and could tolerate a colder climate. We suggested that church congregations go out into their fields to praise God, declaring out His sovereignty over this pest. We understand that where congregations did this in a committed and regular way, they had no further problems with this very destructive worm.

The following year, Pastor Lameck Msamange, leader of the church in Malawi, told me that many churches had continued to praise God in their fields even although there was no longer a problem with the army worm, and where they had done so, the rains had been exceptionally good, so much so that they have differed even from village to village, and chiefs and communities from neighbouring villages had asked the church to come and pray in their fields. News about this demonstration of God's wonderful love, power and presence spread widely throughout the region.

Praise is also a powerful antidote to depression. We hear so often in our news about those who suffer from debilitating depression, even to the point of committing suicide. However, Isaiah tells us that Jesus came to give us *"a garment of praise instead of a spirit of despair."* (Isaiah 61:3 NIV) If we build a habit of praise and worship, it will help us to overcome depression.

I believe that praise and worship is a powerful

weapon with which we can defeat the enemy and turn negative situations into positive ones. As we focus on the wonderful truths included in these devotions instead of the difficulties which we face, we will build our faith in the solution instead of the problem, and through doing so release God's power into our situation.

My suggestion is that we read and meditate on these wonderful biblical truths each morning and take every opportunity during the day to thank God for them, focusing on them instead of the difficulties which we face. As we focus on the many blessings and benefits that we receive in Christ, the truth of them will penetrate deep into our hearts from where they will transform our lives. We hear many sermons about how we should act as believers and I would not undervalue the importance of this teaching. However, I believe passionately that if we can really grasp hold of the truth of the amazing transformation that Jesus achieved for us through His death on the cross, our behavior would automatically change for the better because we will act according to what we believe.

Fri   # Day 1

We are Free to Choose

I call heaven and earth to witness
against you today, that I have set before
you life and death, the blessing and the
curse. So choose life in order that you
may live, you and your descendants,
Deuteronomy 30:19

In the above-quoted verse from Deuteronomy, God offered the Israelites a choice: a choice between life and prosperity or death and destruction. God also offers us the same choice. We can choose how we want to live! He does not force His wonderful presence and blessings upon us. We therefore need to ask ourselves this question: do we want to live with God's continual presence and blessing or do we want to try to live independently? Many of us have tried to make life work through our own efforts and have failed miserably because there are so many factors in life which are beyond our ability to control.

Whenever we buy a piece of technical equipment from a reputable manufacturer, it should come with a book of instructions which show us how this piece of equipment should be used so that we can get the best performance out of it. It will have been written by the firm who designed and made it, and they will know how it was designed to work.

The same is true with God. He created us, and He knows how we can live well. He also promises us in Deuteronomy 30:11-14 that His way is not difficult or beyond our reach or ability. His Word is written to teach us how to live well and when we chose to listen to His advice and to obey His teaching, His presence will enable us to overcome, and even to triumph, in every situation.

This choice between life and prosperity or death and destruction is ours, and ours alone. God's desire is for us to live well but He gives us complete freedom to choose how we want to live. His sovereign power and unlimited resources are available for those who chose to submit to His lordship, and when we put our trust in Him, we will not be disappointed. However, we are free to make this most important decision in our lives: will we choose life or death!

Living Abundantly

*"The thief comes only to steal and kill
and destroy; I came that they may have
life, and have it abundantly."* John 10:10

In the Old Testament, God had offered the Israelites a choice between life and prosperity or death and destruction. In the above-quoted verse from the New Testament, we find Jesus offering us a similar choice with even greater benefits: He said that the thief (Satan) comes to steal, kill and destroy; but He had come so that we may have life, and have it abundantly.

It is important to ask ourselves what Jesus means by living to the full or living abundantly, as written in other translations. The world would understand it to mean living a luxurious lifestyle with great wealth, a large house, a multitude of possessions and a celebrity status. Jesus does not use the word "abundant" in this way for He also warns us to be on our guard against greed, adding that our life does not consist in the abundance of our possessions.

I believe that Jesus is referring to the quality of our life not the quantity of our possessions or our social status. We all want to be loved, happy, peaceful, free, secure, successful, fruitful, strong, courageous, fulfilled and satisfied. We want wealth and possessions because we think that they will give us this quality of life, but they will not. Wealthy people can be the most miserable; often because they have no real purpose in life. Also, if we trust in wealth and possessions, this can make us very insecure because these can be lost, stolen or destroyed. Following Jesus will give us quality of life, wealth and possessions will not.

Jesus demonstrated what a life lived well looks like. He did not have many possessions but the robe that He wore was of good quality. The last three years of His life were lived travelling without even a house to sleep in. However, crowds followed Him because of the authority of His teaching, His power over sickness and even death, His authority over the weather and His ability to multiply food to feed a very large crowd. Incredibly, He promised that we would do even greater things than these if we put our trust in Him.

Day 3

Jesus is Lord

*When He had disarmed the rulers and
authorities, He made a public display of
them, having triumphed over them
through Him.* Colossians 2:15

If we look at New Testament passages where the
gospel message is presented, we find that Peter and
Paul focused almost exclusively on the life, death,
resurrection and exaltation of Jesus. In direct
contrast, our presentation of the gospel is often
focused on ourselves: on how our sins can be
forgiven, our relationship with God restored and the
promise of eternal life through Jesus' sacrificial death
on the cross. This, of course, is all wonderfully true.
However, if we present the gospel in this way, our
focus is on ourselves and we have reduced Jesus to a
commodity.

In this distortion of the gospel, we undermine the
awesome majesty, glory, sovereignty and power of
Jesus. Our focus is on ourselves and not on Him. As a
result, we lose sight of His unequalled ability to
transform and empower our lives, robbing ourselves

of the outworking of His power through us. The reason why the gospel message is such good news is that 'Jesus is Lord'. The gospel accounts of His life show us that He is lord over all sickness, all disability, all evil spirits, all weather conditions and even over death. He is therefore sovereign over everything which controls us, troubles us or opposes us, and this includes our habitual sins and addictions.

The vital importance of this foundational Christian truth led many early Christians to face a horrendous death in the Coliseum in Rome when everyone living under the extensive rule of the Roman empire was required to confess: "Caesar is Lord". This was, of course, abhorrent to Christians who refused in large numbers to do this. As a result, many of them were crucified or fed to lions in the arena with vast crowds watching this barbaric and bloodthirsty spectacle. We can learn from their willingness to die rather than to deny Jesus' lordship, how important they viewed this issue.

Day 4
Every Knee will Bow

*For this reason also, God highly exalted
Him, and bestowed on Him the name
which is above every name, so that at the
name of Jesus EVERY KNEE WILL BOW, of
those who are in heaven and on earth
and under the earth, and that every
tongue will confess that Jesus Christ is
Lord, to the glory of God the Father.*
Philippians 2:9-11

Let us continue with the theme of the Lordship of
Jesus. It was several years ago when I witnessed a
miraculous and tangible demonstration of this
wonderful truth. I was travelling around Uganda with
leaders of different churches. On our final day with
one of these leaders, we visited a location where his
church had been holding an outreach crusade. It was
the final evening of this event. This leader asked his
colleagues how successful this outreach had been.
Their reply was very negative. Apparently, this was
an area which was known to be resistant to the
gospel, very few had attended their meetings and
even less had responded positively to their message.

Only a few people had gathered in that location that

evening. Our Ugandan colleague said that he would preach that evening. His message focused exclusively on the awesome truths about Jesus. He spoke His name in virtually every sentence. Everything he said glorified and exalted Jesus. About half the way through his message, I heard what sounded like a clap of thunder. Soon after this people started to join us, and the number steadily increased until there was a large crowd all standing around the raised stage. When an altar call was given, most of that large crowd surged forward.

This was a tangible demonstration of the awesome power and sovereignty of Jesus. When we focus our attention on Him, declaring out the truth of His exaltation, victory and glory, the powers of evil are overcome. I believe that the clap of thunder marked the moment when the evil powers which had held this area in bondage for so many years were broken by the awesome power of the name of our wonderful Lord and Saviour.

Day 5

God chooses the Weak

*...but God has chosen the foolish things of
the world to shame the wise, and God has
chosen the weak things of the world to
shame the things which are strong, and
the base things of the world and the
despised God has chosen, the things that
are not, so that He may nullify the things
that are, so that no man may boast
before God.* 1 Corinthians 1:27-29

Those of us who have applied for a job will know
that employers will ask for details of our education,
training, job experience, and character before
employing us. If you have never applied for a job,
consider how you would choose a church leader:
surely you would choose a person who has
demonstrated the qualifications for this role.

However, God's way of choosing workers is quite the
opposite: He chooses the foolish, weak, lowly and
despised people, rather than the strong and highly
educated. He does this because the weak and foolish
know that they need to depend on His ability rather
than their own and will therefore give Him the glory
for everything that He enables them to do. A better

qualified person is more likely to take the glory for himself. It is also true that foolish people will know their need to learn God's ways. In direct contrast, those who are well educated and talented are far more likely to trust in their own ability and act according to their own plans and desires. Furthermore, confident and wealthy people often trust in their own abilities and resources, which are very limited, and therefore fail to draw upon God's unlimited resources.

The truth is that no-one is beyond the reach of God's love, help and favour. It does not matter who we are or what we have done. Even those who have committed the most heinous sins are not exempted. Jesus told His disciples that He had chosen them, they had not chosen Him. This is also true for us. We should never disqualify ourselves or under-estimate our ability to serve God, for our success does not depend on our ability but on His.

Day 6
God's Unconditional Love

But God demonstrates His own love toward us, in that while we were yet sinners, Christ died for us. Roman 5:8

One of the most basic needs that we all have as human beings is to be loved, accepted and respected. This need to be loved is so strong that we can put considerably time and effort into creating an outward image of being attractive, confident and successful even though this image can be in direct contrast to how we feel inside.

Freedom from this desperate need to earn love comes through the knowledge that God loves us unconditionally. The wonderful truth is that God's love for us is not changed by our appearance, performance or behaviour. In direct contrast to human love, God's love is not dependent on the performance or quality of the object of His love but on the nature and character of God Himself.

Today's reading shows the nature of God's unconditional love for every one of us: it was while we were still sinners that Jesus died for us. When Jesus went to the cross, we were all alienated from

God and in rebellion against His just laws and decrees. We had done nothing whatsoever to show ourselves worthy of His love and yet God still sent His Son to die on the cross so that our sins could be forgiven and our relationship with Him restored.

Our value is based on the wonderful truth that God created us, and that Jesus has not only redeemed us, but has also credited us with His righteousness. Just as the value of a painting, even a damaged one, is based on the reputation of the artist who painted it, so our value is based on our creator and not on our appearance or performance. When we truly understand how much we are deeply and unconditionally loved by God, it will change absolutely everything. It is, perhaps, the most life-transforming revelation that we can receive, and I believe that it can only be given to us by God Himself. Let us therefore pray that God will open our hearts to receive this priceless gift: a revelation of His unconditional love for us.

Day 7

God's Extravagant Love

*See how great a love the Father has
bestowed on us, that we would be called
children of God; and such we are. For this
reason the world does not know us,
because it did not know Him.* 1 John 3:1

I recently heard a sermon illustration which described God's love in a very effective way. The speaker was describing how he had travelled to France with a group of friends from his time at university and how one of these friends worked for a well-known brand of chocolate. She had therefore taken with her a very large quantity of chocolates for everyone in the group to enjoy throughout their stay. He went on to describe how there were so many chocolates of every kind and filling, that everyone in the group could eat as many as they liked and of the variety which they preferred without any concern that their own favourite would run out.

He contrasted this extravagant supply of chocolate with how he and his wife would occasionally buy some chocolate for the family to enjoy while watching television in the evening. However, in this situation, they only bought one bar and so the sections of chocolate had to be carefully counted and the total divided exactly into four equal parts.

He went on to say that we, as believers, often treat God's love in the same way as his family's small supply of chocolate. We compete or judge or criticise each other, trying to be better in order to gain God's love. Alternatively, we struggle and strive in order to earn His love. Whereas, in direct contrast, God's love is more like the abundant supply that this speaker had seen in France. His love is extravagant and totally unlimited. We can never exhaust His supply and we certainly do not need to earn it or to compete with others in order to receive it. Tragically, when we fail to comprehend the inexhaustible supply of God's love, our competitive and performance-based behaviour leads us to focus on self instead of God, robbing us of a revelation of this life-changing truth.

Day 8

God's Treasured Possession

"For you are a people holy to the LORD your God. The LORD your God has chosen you out of all the peoples on the face of the earth to be his people, his treasured possession." Deuteronomy 7:6 (NIV)

One of our most basic human needs is to feel valued and secure, and we were created to find these in God, Himself. The sin which all of us is guilty of is that of living independently from Him, and through doing so we deny ourselves these peace-giving necessities of life. We may seek to mask these unmet needs through acquiring great wealth, taking out insurance, striving to lift ourselves socially, or buying expensive possessions and clothing, but nothing short of a deep faith and trust in God can give us what we crave for.

This verse tells us that we are God's treasured possession. Let us consider how we, even as flawed human beings, would care for an item which we treasure: surely, we would keep it somewhere safe. We would also put it in a place where it is on display to others. I would liken it to a priceless ornament kept in a glass-fronted display cabinet where it is both protected but also visible for visitors to admire.

This verse gives us a picture of how God wants to care for us and to put us on display to a hurting world. We all know that God does not always protect us from all danger. Jesus warned that we would face trouble in this world. He does, however, give us the inner strength to cope with every situation which we face if we place our trust in Him. I have found through many experiences, that when life gets hard, God just lifts me up and carries me. He will also protect our hearts with His peace and Jesus confirms that God wants to display us where the world can see our good deeds and give the glory to Him.

> *"You are the light of the world. A city set on a hill cannot be hidden; nor does anyone light a lamp and put it under a basket, but on the lampstand, and it gives light to all who are in the house. Let your light shine before men in such a way that they may see your good works, and glorify your Father who is in heaven."* Matthew 5:14-16.

Day 9

God Will Carry Us

*"and in the wilderness where you saw
how the LORD your God carried you, just
as a man carries his son, in all the way
which you have walked until you came to
this place."* Deuteronomy 1:31

I was praying for a friend when I saw a picture of God cradling her in His arms. He told me that she was about to go through a difficult time but that He would carry her through it. I saw weeds and thistles on the ground, but she was being held above them so that they did not hurt her. Upon sharing this picture and my understanding of what it meant, this lady started to cry. She told us that she had woken up during the previous night feeling a pain in her breast, and upon looking in the bathroom mirror had found a lump. She had just made an appointment to see her doctor the following day. This revelation of God's care enabled her to walk through her treatment without any fear.

This event caused me to reflect on the scripture passages which speak about God carrying His people. I asked myself why we so often deny ourselves this promised help. One reason is that we want to stay in control of our lives. In direct contrast, if we allow anyone to carry us, we can no longer control the direction which we take. When God carries us, we will be taken where He goes.

Ezekiel 47 describes a vision of water flowing from the temple and him being led through water of different depths. This vision is said to describe the flow of the Holy Spirit through our lives. When we walk through ankle-deep water, we can control where we go but when we are out of our depth, we will be carried by the flow of the Holy Spirit. Similarly, when God carries us, we cannot control where we go as our feet are not on the ground.

I have known times when God has carried me. It happens when circumstances are very hard and God takes over, making a very difficult situation easy. When circumstances get harder, I have reached a point where suddenly everything gets easy even although the circumstances have not improved. If we reflect on this wonderful truth, it should be a wonderful antidote to fear and anxiety.

Day 10
Treasure in Earthen Vessels

*But we have this treasure in earthen
vessels, so that the surpassing greatness
of the power will be of God and not from
ourselves; we are afflicted in every way,
but not crushed; perplexed, but not
despairing; persecuted, but not forsaken;
struck down, but not destroyed;*
2 Corinthians 4:7-9

This passage describes how the very powerful presence of God within us will enable us to cope with any circumstance, however hard. One picture which describes this wonderful truth well is of a flimsy carboard box. If it is empty and then hit just once with a light cane, it will be crushed immediately. However, if it is then filled with solid concrete, no weapon – however powerful or however sustained the attack – will be able to cause it to collapse.

If our focus is on the frailty of our physical body or the instability of our emotions, then the unpredictability of life will cause us considerable anxiety and fear. However, if we focus instead on the indwelling power of the Holy Spirit and God's numerous promises to protect us and care for us, then we can live in peace even when facing tests and trials of various kinds.

In James 1, this author tells us to consider it all joy when we face trials of many kinds because testing will make us mature, not lacking anything. There are also other similar promises of the benefits of hardship and suffering. Testing will encourage us to seek and to find this inner strength within us. When circumstances are hard and we reach the end of our own resources, we can choose not to trust any longer in our very limited ability to protect ourselves, and thus discover the wonderful truth of this treasure within us.

Once circumstances have led us to transfer our trust from ourselves and to God, everything will change. We will begin to discover the all-surpassing power and unlimited resources of God's indwelling presence. Anxiety and fear will go, and we will be enabled to step out into difficult situations as and when God leads us to do so, knowing that He will enable us to live victoriously.

Day 11
More that Conquerors

But in all these things we
overwhelmingly conquer through Him
who loved us. Romans 8:37

Let us continue with the theme of how we see ourselves. We find a typical example of how many of us perceive ourselves in Numbers, chapter thirteen, when Moses sent the twelve spies to investigate the land of Canaan. You may remember that only Joshua and Caleb came back with a positive report, while the remaining ten spies perceived themselves from a very negative viewpoint. They reported that the inhabitants of the land were of great size while they saw themselves as grasshoppers. This is how many of us perceive ourselves: as smaller, weaker, less attractive and less significant than those around us.

It is of vital importance that we see ourselves as the Bible describes those who are in Christ Jesus. There are many scriptures that speak of our position in Christ and the verse quoted above is just one of many. We perhaps need to remind ourselves that immediately we ask Jesus to become our Lord and Saviour, everything changes. As Paul wrote in his second letter to the church in Corinth, chapter five, we have become a new creature and the old has gone.

This is one area where our minds need to be renewed. I like the tradition in many convents and monasteries where those who join an order are given a new name. A new name, I believe, symbolises and reminds us of the truth of our transformation. An alternative plan would be to choose to change how we speak about ourselves – whether we initially believe it or not. We find a good example of this in John, the disciple: in so many passages in the gospel which he wrote, he refers to himself as the disciple who Jesus loves.

I recommend that we follow his example. We can start by using the verse quoted above in praise and worship as follows:

> *Thank you, Lord, that you have transformed me into a completely new creature and made me to be more than a conqueror. I choose not to focus on my weaknesses and failures, but on your powerful presence within me. I am not weak; I am more than a conqueror.*

Day 12
Nothing is Impossible

"For nothing will be impossible with God." Luke 1:37

When we make Jesus our Lord and Saviour, nothing – within the confines of His plans and purposes for our life – will be impossible. God's indwelling and very powerful presence can work within us and flow through us to others. We are no longer restricted to our self-perceived plans and very limited human effort and strength, and our lives can become prosperous and successful. However, there is a cost involved. If we want to see God's power flowing through us, we need to learn to partner with Him and to do things His way. Isaiah tells us that God's thoughts and ways are different from ours, and it is us who needs to change! In my experience, the cost is negligible when compared with the thrill, fulfilment and joy of walking with Him.

I have had the privilege of seeing miracles like those we read about in the pages of our Bibles. I have seen eight small boxes of clothing multiplied so that about 1,000 people each received two items. Four boxes remained unopened. I know a pastor in Africa whose half bag of maize flour fed about twenty visiting church members for a month. The level of flour did not go down until after they had left. I have been healed and rescued on numerous occasions and was enabled to escape from flooding in a journey that would compare well with any James Bond movie, to name just a few. However, my experiences are few and undramatic when compared with the testimony of many others.

Sadly, our very limited expectations of what God can achieve through us often robs us of the awesome benefits and blessings of His indwelling presence. We can have such a poor opinion of ourselves and our potential in Christ. Alternatively, we are over-confident in our abilities and try to achieve things without Him. Let us therefore look again at the many events in the Bible where God worked very powerfully through people who would seem weak and insignificant in the eyes of the world. Mary being just one example of many. Then, let us thank God that He is the same yesterday, today and forever, and that He wants His miraculous power to flow through us to a hurting world.

Day 13
Plans to prosper Us

"For I know the plans that I have for
you,' declares the LORD, *'plans for welfare*
and not for calamity to give you a future
and a hope." Jeremiah 29:11

Let us consider the kind of plans that most human parents have for their children. Surely, they want the very best for them and will do everything possible to provide them with the very best education and training that will equip them for a prosperous, happy and fulfilled future. One often hears news stories of parents who are even prepared the expense and inconvenience of moving to a different location in order that their children can attend the best school. Many will also be prepared to go without small luxuries for themselves in order that they can provide the finances necessary for extra lessons and/or training. How can we therefore think that God's plans for us, His children, are in any way inferior to those of flawed and often selfish human beings.

The above verse from Jeremiah confirms that God plans are to prosper us and to give us hope and a future. He loves us and wants the very best for us. I believe that He lovingly plans and prepares for our future and is delighted when He sees us do well. He also knows us far better than we know ourselves and will plan a future that is perfect in every way for us, as an individual. This has been my experience. God has led me to do things that I would never have even dreamed of for myself, and these plans have given me so much joy and fulfilment. I have also discovered skills that I did not know I had.

There is a further truth that we should also consider today. When we follow God's plans for our life, He will not only provide us with all the skills which we need, He will also open doors and provide all the necessary finances which will enable us to fulfil these plans. Once again, this has been my experience. I have sometimes stood open-mouthed in amazement at the many miraculous ways that doors have opened, contacts have been made and finances have been provided. Very few of which I could have done for myself. Furthermore, when God puts us in a position, He will also maintain that position for us.

Day 14

Under His Wings

"Jerusalem, Jerusalem, who kills the prophets and stones those who are sent to her! How often I wanted to gather your children together, the way a hen gathers her chicks under her wings, and you were unwilling." Matthew 23:37.

It was a few years ago when I heard a reportedly true story which brings tears to my eyes every time that I think of it. This story told of a man who was walking through a wood which had very recently been burnt to the ground. Everything in that location appeared to be reduced to charred wood and ashes. Then he came upon a bird which was also charred like the rest of the landscape. He touched it gently with his foot and four live chicks ran from underneath her charred body. This bird could, of course, have flown away and thus escaped the fire but her chicks could not. She had apparently chosen to be burnt alive in order to protect her chicks. The picture of her sitting there without moving as the flames consumed her, moves me to tears. This above-quoted verse from Matthew always reminds me of this story. What a wonderful picture this is of how Jesus chose to suffer an extremely painful death in order to save us. He could have saved Himself, but He chose to die.

However, there is even more to this very moving story. The preparedness of this bird to die in order to protect her chicks, reminds us of the loving and protective heart that most mothers – both human and animal – have for their young: a love and protective instinct that has been given to them by God Himself. Because of the weakness and vulnerability of all new-borns, God created all mothers to have this self-sacrificing instinct to care for and to protect their young regardless of the cost. It follows therefore, that if God created mothers with this protective love, this must be a picture of how He loves and protects us. Furthermore, He demonstrated this love by sending His own dearly beloved Son to die on our behalf. The tragedy of Jesus' words is that the Israelites had not allowed God to care for them in this way. Do we? Let us meditate on this story and allow God's love to penetrate our hearts.

Day 15

A Robe of Righteousness

*I will rejoice greatly in the LORD, My soul
will exult in my God; For He has clothed me
with garments of salvation, He has
wrapped me with a robe of righteousness,
as a bridegroom decks himself with a
garland, and as a bride adorns herself with
her jewels.* Isaiah 61:10

Many of us continue to struggle with sins which have controlled us for many years, despite knowing the wonderful truth that Jesus' death on the cross has set us free from the power and control of sin. We can therefore feel very frustrated, knowing that our life experience does not match the truth of the gospel. With this in mind, I am learning that the quality of our Christian life is very often dependant on how we see ourselves: if we see ourselves as weak, sinful, selfish and poor, we will live weak, sinful, selfish and poverty-stricken lives. In direct contrast, if we see ourselves as a completely new creature in Christ and that our old self has gone, then our life will be transformed.

It was some time ago when God gave me a picture relating to our struggle with repeated sin. It has helped me, and I believe that it will also help others. He brought the truth of this verse from Isaiah to my attention. He said that if I could really grasp hold of this wonderful life-changing truth: that He has arrayed me in a robe of His righteousness, then I would find it relatively easy to resist sin. He showed me a picture of me wearing a spotlessly white wedding dress and asked me whether I would go into a coal cellar to fetch coal if I was dressed in this way. I responded that I would not. He then showed me that if I was wearing dirty jeans, I would not think twice about doing so.

I probably do not need to explain how we should apply this picture to our lives. If we see ourselves as clothed in a spotlessly white robe of His righteousness, and thank Him for not only forgiving us for our sins but also crediting us with all the righteous deeds of Jesus, then we will not want to dirty our spotless appearance, and resisting sin will become comparatively easy. However, if we see ourselves as weak and sinful, and we know that that Satan constantly condemns us, one more sin will not appear to make any difference.

Day 16
Christ has set Us Free

It was for freedom that Christ set us free;
therefore keep standing firm and do not be
subject again to a yoke of slavery.
Galatians 5:1

Paul is speaking here about freedom from the Law. He goes on to say that if they submit to circumcision, they will need to obey the whole Law and will be alienated from Christ. When we are in Christ, we are set free from the rules and regulations of the Law. This is good news. However, freedom – written in this context - does not mean living independently. We were not created to live independently from God, and if we try to do so, we will find ourselves controlled by the world, the flesh and the devil – the forces who oppose us.

This, I believe, is why so many of us continue to struggle with sin, even though we confess to have made Jesus our Lord and Saviour. Paul explains in his letter to the Romans, chapter eight, that it is when we are led by the Spirit that we are set free from the law of sin and death. When we try to live independently from God, we will be limited to our own strength and resources and will be no match against the spiritual forces of evil who wage war against us. It is only as we submit ourselves to God, that we are empowered to resist evil.

Let us look at this truth in the form of a parable. If we consider the heavenly battle between good and evil, we - as a lone independent soldier - will be quickly annihilated by the forces of evil. However, if we enlist into God's army, and enlisting into any army always requires submitting to the authorities of that army, we will be surrounded, protected and empowered by God's far superior forces. This truth is confirmed in James 4:7 where he teaches us to submit ourselves to God before trying to resist the devil. As the focus of this whole chapter is on sin, we should interpret this verse from this perspective. It is only when we submit ourselves to God that the devil will obey our command to flee. If each time we are tempted to sin, we submit ourselves to God – not just with words as we so often do, but with genuine humility and a commitment to obedience, then we will be empowered to resist all temptation.

Day 17

Jesus will help Us

Because he himself suffered when he was tempted, he is able to help those who are being tempted ... For we do not have a high priest who is unable to feel sympathy for our weaknesses, but we have one who has been tempted in every way, just as we are – yet he did not sin.
Hebrew 2:18; 4:15 (NIV)

We can find at least three very significant truths in these two verses. First, it is because Jesus was tempted, but did not sin, that He is able to help us when we are tempted. If we need help to perform any task, it is always advisable to speak to someone who has experience in that area and has demonstrated an ability to fulfil that task to a high standard. Jesus has demonstrated His ability to resist and to overcome temptation and He can therefore help us to do so.

Second, the writer tells us that Jesus was tempted in every way as we are. This is an amazing truth which emphasises that Jesus was fully human as well as fully God. It is easy for us to imagine incorrectly that Jesus was only half human and did not, therefore, face constant temptation in the way that we do. Also, we can wrongly presume that He did not face the more extreme temptations that confront many of us: the kind of temptations that we are so ashamed of that we would not even tell our best friend about them. These two verses therefore teach us that however ashamed we are of the nature of some of the temptations that we experience, we can share them with Jesus, knowing that he will sympathise with us and will not criticise us or judge us.

Third, the writer tells us that Jesus suffered when He was tempted. This shows us that He knows how hard it can be to resist some temptations. He will not, therefore, criticise or judge us when we have given in to temptation, and we do not need to feel too ashamed to ask for His help when have allowed any sin to dominate or control us. When we rightly focus on the perfection of Jesus, we can doubt His ability to sympathise with our failures. These two verses show us that this presumption is contrary to the wonderful truth. However, heinous the nature of our sin, Jesus will sympathise with us and help us.

Day 18
Living Triumphantly

... for the accuser of our brethren has
been thrown down, he who accuses them
before our God day and night. And they
overcame him because of the blood of the
Lamb and because of the word of their
testimony, and they did not love their life
even when faced with death.
Revelation 12:10b-11

There are so many verses in the New Testament which speak of our victory in Christ. We know that the early believers faced horrendous persecution and suffering, and yet after the coming of the Holy Spirit, there is no hint of any of them living defeated lives. When facing death by stoning, Stephen – who was full of the Holy Spirit - saw heaven open before him and forgave those who had ordered his death, just as Jesus had done. After being beaten with rods, severely flogged, and thrown into a prison cell with their feet in stocks, Paul and Silas prayed and sang hymns to God. There were also many believers who chose to die in the Colosseum in Rome rather than deny the Lordship of Jesus.

These above-quoted verses tell us that Satan had accused the believers before God day and night, but they had triumphed over him by the blood of the Lamb and by the word of their testimony. Satan, of course, has not yet been thrown down and therefore continues to accuse us. These verses help us to understand his tactics and through doing so, to triumph over him as these early believers had. In the context of these verses, Satan's weapon was accusation. He undermines our righteous position in Christ through reminding us of our failures and weaknesses, and through doing this he achieves two objectives:

First, through making us feel guilty, he gets our eyes onto ourselves. We focus on our sins and weaknesses and lose sight of God's awesome sovereignty, mercy and power. We live victorious lives when our focus is on God. Second, when we focus on our weaknesses and failures, we will live weak and defeated lives. How we see ourselves will have dramatic consequences in our lives. We triumph over Satan through testifying that the blood of Jesus continually cleanses us from every sin and failure and he no longer has any hold over us.

Day 19

We have been Chosen

*"You did not choose Me but I chose you,
and appointed you that you would go
and bear fruit, and that your fruit would
remain, so that whatever you ask of the
Father in My name He may give to you."*
John 15:16

I do not know what memories you have of your childhood. Mine was not very positive either at home or at school. I clearly remember three different experiences, two at school and one at home, which I found very painful. First, during many sporting activities at school, two leaders – who were good at sport - were chosen and they had to pick their teams. They took it in turns to choose from the rest of us until no-one was left. I was always one of the last ones to be chosen because I was not very good at sport. Second, we had to go for a walk each week with one other person. We therefore had to find someone to walk with. As I had no special friend, I always found this difficult as no-one chose to walk with me. Third, as an older teenager, I went to local dances and remember the pain of standing at the edge of the dancefloor waiting in vain for someone to ask me to dance. Can you can relate to this kind of rejection?

These above-quoted words of Jesus therefore speak very powerfully to me. In direct contrast to my past, they make me feel very special, and my experience as a believer has confirmed that they are true in two important ways. First, God has clearly led me into a very exciting and powerful ministry in Africa: a ministry which I could never have organised for myself and in which we have seen a continual demonstration of His presence and power. Second, I have hundreds, possibly thousands, of friends and work-colleagues many of whom regularly communicate appreciation for our friendship.

Jesus explained how He searches for us in two parables which are recorded in the gospel of Luke, chapter fifteen. They are the well-known parables of the lost sheep and the lost coin. In both these parables, the emphasis is on the lengths that the shepherd and woman went to in order to find the sheep and coin which had been lost. This gives us a wonderful picture of the lengths that God goes to in order to find us. We did not choose Him, He chose us.

Day 20
Seated with Christ

...and raised us up with Him, and seated
us with Him in the heavenly places in
Christ Jesus,... Ephesians 2:6

It is difficult for us to fully comprehend, let alone believe, the incomparable blessings and benefits that God offers us in Christ. This, I believe, is why so many of us live frustrated, unfruitful, anxious and sometimes defeated lives. This above-quoted verse is just one of many where Paul describes our current position as new covenant believers. However, although we may recognise that God has exalted and glorified Jesus, the almost unbelievable fact that we are seated with Him in heavenly places is difficult for us fully embrace.

This verse does not, of course, describe the current location of our physical bodies. Rather it is describing our position of spiritual authority and our access to all the heavenly resources which are available to Jesus. I am increasingly convinced that our victory and fruitfulness as believers depends far more on what we believe than on what we do. So much of our focus can be on our performance and achievements, and especially on our failure to achieve our goals and desires and the consequent decisions to try even harder in future. All this can be very frustrating and demoralising.

The more we focus on our failures and efforts to try harder, the greater our failure to achieve our goals and desires. We have already considered two reasons why this is so, but there are two more. First, our focus will be on self and not on God. Second, when we focus on our failures, we will live defeated lives. Third, we will see ourselves under our problems instead of above them. Fourth, we are trying reach heavenly goals from an earthly position.

Jesus promised us an abundant life, but it cannot be lived from a worldly position. We can spend our life trying unsuccessfully to climb a ladder to reach our goals, only to find that God had already put us on the top rung. All our time and effort has therefore been wasted in the climbing process, when we could have spent that time bearing fruit which can only be reached from the top.

Day 21

In the Heavenly Realms

...and raised us up with Him, and seated
us with Him in the heavenly places in
Christ Jesus,... Ephesians 2:6

We will spend one further day considering this same verse from Ephesians. The key phrase in this verse is that God has raised us up. The moment that we ask Jesus to be our Lord and saviour, we are raised up with Him and given the same position of spiritual authority as He has been given, even although our physical bodies remain temporarily on earth. It is the fact that our bodies remain on earth that can confuse us, leading us to think, speak and act from an earthly position and seeing ourselves as small, weak and inferior.

There are many negative consequences of our failing to grasp hold of our true position in Christ. We will consider just three of them today. First, as we mentioned briefly yesterday: if we fail to understand our true spiritual position, we can be overwhelmed by the problems which continually confront us because instead of looking at them from a place of spiritual authority, we look at them from a weak, vulnerable, defeated and inferior position.

We also mentioned the second consequence yesterday. We will look at it from a different perspective today. Because we see ourselves in a lowly position, many of us spend our lives trying to lift ourselves to a place where we think that we can achieve more for God and gain some social status. However, in Luke 14, Jesus warned us that when we do this, God will humble us. In direct contrast, when we recognise our raised position, we will be able to humble ourselves, and when we do so, Jesus tells us that God will exalt us.

Third, when we live from our heavenly position with Christ, this should build faith and confidence in our eternal destiny. As we continually look at life from a heavenly position, we should increasingly see heaven as our true home. It will also help us to view life from a more truthful perspective: that earth – with all its pain and suffering – is only our temporary home, and heaven – where there will be no more mourning, crying or pain – is our eternal destiny.

Day 22
Power from on High

"And behold, I am sending forth the
promise of My Father upon you; but you
are to stay in the city until you are
clothed with power from on high."
Luke 24:49

I wonder how you would describe yourself. Very few of us, I believe, would refer to ourselves as powerful. We are confronted daily with situations over which we feel that we have very little control. Life often appears difficult, stressful and unjust. Each day can sometimes be a struggle and however hard we try; our goals and desires often appear more and more unobtainable.

The truth is that we were not created to live independently. We were created according to God's plan: to live in close relationship with Him and dependent on His presence and help. In the above-quoted verse, Jesus told His disciples to wait in the city until they had received power from on high. Jesus knew that without His indwelling power, they would not be able to fulfil His mission to evangelise the world, nor would they have the inner strength and courage to stand up to the severe persecution that would soon follow.

We see a good example of this after Jesus was crucified: all the disciples – who had been specifically chosen by God - were terrified and hid in fear of their lives. The contrast after the Day of Pentecost could not be more extreme: from a place of hiding, they stood boldly and publicly to declare the wonderful truth about Jesus despite the severe persecution that started almost immediately.

They were not only set free from fear, but their God-inspired and anointed words convicted thousands who came into the kingdom in vast numbers. Many were also healed and throughout the book of Acts, we read of miraculous demonstrations of God's presence and power. These were the same men who had been hiding in fear just a short time earlier. These disciples were ordinary men, and most were uneducated. Surely, if the indwelling Holy Spirit could transform and empower their lives and make them fruitful, He can transform and empower us. The question is: do we ask Him and expect Him to do so?

Day 23

Even Greater Things

*"Truly, truly, I say to you, he who believes
in Me, the works that I do, he will do also;
and greater works than these he will do;
because I go to the Father."* John 14:12

We considered yesterday how the Holy Spirit transformed the lives of the disciples and empowered them to be both courageous and fruitful. Within just a short period of time they were transformed from hiding in fear of their lives to speaking publicly and effectively about Jesus, leading vast crowds into the kingdom and seeing miraculous demonstrations of God's presence and power.

This powerful, courageous, miraculous and fruitful life, as demonstrated by the early believers, should be normal Christianity, and not the exception! There is no indication in the Bible, that these demonstrations of God's presence and power should finish at the end of the first century. Furthermore, in the above-quoted verse, Jesus tells us that we will be able to do even greater works than He had done because He was going to His Father.

There are, of course, present day testimonies of God

performing a whole variety of wonderful miracles. Sadly, however, these testimonies are perceived as unusual, rather than normal Christianity! We need, therefore, to ask ourselves why Christianity is so different now from that experienced by these early believers. Let us consider just one of many reasons why we so often fail to see a fulfilment of this amazing promise given to us by Jesus Himself.

One answer lies in what we perceive to be normal Christianity. Do we expect to see a demonstration of God's power on a day-to-day basis? The disciples had one great advantage over us: they had spent three years with Jesus and had been present when so many miracles were demonstrated; so much so that miracles would have become a new normal for them. Later they saw miracles because they expected to see miracles. In direct contrast, we seldom see miracles because we do not expect to see them. One solution for us would be to meditate on the gospels stories until miracles become a new normal for us.

Day 24

Every Blessing

*Blessed be the God and Father of our
Lord Jesus Christ, who has blessed us
with every spiritual blessing in the
heavenly places in Christ...*
Ephesians 1:3

It is difficult to find adequate words to describe the awesome benefits and blessings which God gives us in Christ. They are even more astonishing when we consider our position before God poured His life-transforming power and mercy into our lives. Later in this same letter, Paul wrote that we were dead in our transgressions and sins, following the way of this world and its ruler - Satan, gratifying the cravings of our flesh and deserving of wrath.

Incredibly, instead of wrath we have received mercy, and instead of the death sentence we have received every possible blessing which is available in the heavenly realms. I believe that this means that every resource which was available to Jesus is now available to us. Furthermore, this wonderful truth is supported by the words of Jesus which we considered yesterday.

Let us consider this truth in the form of a parable: we have been taken to court to be tried for a sin, the legal punishment for which would be a life sentence without parole. We are therefore standing in the dock and God, Himself, is the judge. Let us try to picture this scene so that it becomes more real to us. The case against us is presented and proven beyond any reasonable doubt. The jury unanimously find us guilty. We wait in fear for the judge to proclaim the expected penalty which would mean spending the rest of our life in prison.

As expected, the judge declares us guilty. He then steps down from the judge's chair and takes His place beside us in the dock declaring that He, Himself, will take our punishment and that we are completely free to go. Not only are we free to go, but He also tells us that our police record will be deleted and that He has imputed to us every benefit that has been available to Him because of His position of authority and honour as a judge. This is what God has done for us. Not only has Jesus taken the punishment for our sin, but every heavenly blessing and benefit which He enjoyed is now available to us.

Day 25

Open our Eyes

So he answered, "Do not fear, for those who are with us are more than those who are with them." Then Elisha prayed and said, "O LORD, I pray, open his eyes that he may see." And the LORD opened the servant's eyes and he saw; and behold, the mountain was full of horses and chariots of fire all around Elisha. 2 Kings 6:16-17

This story of Elisha serves as a very graphic reminder of this wonderful truth: the forces of God, who are with us, are far greater than the forces of Satan, who oppose us. In this story we read that a vast army with horses and chariots had surrounded the city and so Elisha's servant asked him what they should do. In direct contrast to his servant who was only looking at the forces who had come against them, Elisha was able to see the more numerous and far superior heavenly forces who were surrounding them to protect them.

Whenever we face opposition, we should remember this story of Elisha. It will help us to put our trials into correct perspective: we may face trouble, sickness, difficulty, opposition, slander, injustice, and/or abuse, but the wonderful truth is that however many forces of evil come against us, God will surround us with far greater and infinitely more powerful forces to care for us and to protect us.

Sadly, we can be like Elisha's servant and focus solely on the opposition which confronts us. Through doing this, we can draw the false conclusion that the forces ranged against us are greater than those which are ready to protect us. God allows us to face hardship and opposition, but He does not leave us to face it alone and His power is far greater that any forces which come against us.

Many years ago, I experienced troubling dreams, waking up with a sense of darkness and fear. Then God brought this truth to my attention: there are far more angels around me when I sleep than there are forces of darkness to attack me. Satan can work in a variety of different ways to oppose us, but the spiritual forces which surround us are significantly more powerful. Like Elisha, let us pray that God will open our eyes to this wonderful truth.

Day 26

The Lord is my Shepherd

The LORD is my shepherd, I lack nothing.
Psalm 23:1 (NIV)

Jesus, Himself confirmed these words of the psalmist. In the gospel of John, He described Himself as the good shepherd who lays his life down for his sheep. He added that a hired man does not own or love the sheep and therefore abandons them and runs away when a wolf comes to attack them.

If we are to understand the significance of the psalmist's words, we should remember that sheep are helpless and vulnerable animals. They are not able to defend themselves against predators and often walk into danger, such as falling down a crevice. They are also vulnerable to an infestation of parasites. Unlike other animals, they need a good shepherd to look after them.

The Bible uses the symbolism of sheep to describe us because we are helpless and vulnerable like they are. Just as predators, such as wolves, attacked sheep in Jesus' day, so the world in which we live is full of dangers and temptations which we do not always recognise and from which we need to be protected.

Without God's constant guidance and care we can so easily walk into situations which are destructive, dangerous, addictive or predatorial.

There are two reasons why we often fail to avail ourselves of God's promised guidance and protection. First, we are reluctant to recognise our inability to look after ourselves. We want to live independently and to take control of our own lives. We can also be proud and unteachable. We deceive ourselves that we do not need someone else to show us how to live well.

Second, our experience of living in a fallen world has taught us of the danger of depending on others, and so we find it hard to put our lives into someone else's hands. This may be why God repeatedly tells us that He loves us and will care for us; using a variety of symbolisms to describe Himself so that we will trust Him. He is the good shepherd who will not fail us or forsake us. The psalmist goes on to tell us that when we allow God to shepherd us, we will not lack anything: no genuine need, therefore, will remain unmet.

Day 27
For the Joy

*...fixing our eyes on Jesus, the author
and perfecter of faith, who for the joy
set before Him endured the cross,
despising the shame, and has sat
down at the right hand of the throne
of God.* Hebrews 12:2

In this above-quoted verse, the writer of the letter to the Hebrews tells us that it was because of the joy set before Him that Jesus endured the cross. One example of the meaning of this phrase would be the birth of a baby. A woman endures the pain – and in the past, danger - of childbirth knowing that she will soon experience the joy of having a baby. The expectation of a child outweighs the pain and danger of childbirth. With this understanding in mind, there are two helpful and encouraging truths that we can gain from this verse.

First, it was for the joy of restoring His broken relationship with us that led Jesus to the cross. We know from the accounts of Jesus praying in the Garden of Gethsemane that this decision was not forced upon Him and that He was tempted not to go through with it. We could presume that it was out of a sense of duty and in order to be obedient to His father that He made this very difficult decision. He was, of course, always obedient to His Father but there was a different reason given for His choice: it was for the joy, presumably of restoring our broken relationship with God. This truth should give us an even greater understanding of how much He loves us. He loves us so much that the joy of being re-united with us outweighed the extreme pain of crucifixion.

Second, we can learn from the choice which Jesus made, for it is living a self-sacrificing life for the benefit of others - as Jesus did - that will give us the greatest joy. This teaching is given throughout the pages of the Bible, but it has also been my own experience. We are all tempted to be self-focused and self-serving. However, I find that when I focus on self and on what I can purchase or achieve for my own benefit, whatever I buy or achieve is never enough. I always need one more thing or one more achievement! My greatest and most sustained joy has always been through loving and serving others.

Day 28

Sharing His Glory

...and if children, heirs also, heirs of God and fellow heirs with Christ, if indeed we suffer with Him so that we may also be glorified with Him. For I consider that the sufferings of this present time are not worthy to be compared with the glory that is to be revealed to us. Romans 8:17-18

Many biblical truths are contrary to our worldly way of thinking. Our natural goal would be to avoid all pain and suffering. However, Paul tells us that if we share in Jesus' sufferings, we will also share in His glory. This is not a message that we want to hear, and, in fact, I cannot remember when I last heard a message on suffering or sacrifice. We seem to prefer a sanitised version of the gospel, focusing on the promised blessings and benefits and leaving out the cost of a genuine commitment to Jesus. However, if we sanitise the gospel in this way, we render it powerless. Jesus never supported this restricted view of the gospel and His teaching emphasised the necessary cost of discipleship.

The truth is that we receive the blessings and benefits

promised in the gospel through death to our self-life. In Philippians 3, Paul expressed a desire to participate in Jesus' suffering and to become like Him in His death. However, this was his desire, not his goal. His goal was to know the power of Jesus' resurrection and to attain to the resurrection from the dead. Paul understood this important truth: that it is through identifying with Jesus' death, that we are empowered to live a resurrection life.

In Galatians chapter 2, Paul declared that he had been crucified with Christ and that he no longer lived but Christ lived in him. In the sixth chapter of his letter to the Romans, he wrote that if we are united with Jesus in his death, we will also be untied with Him in His resurrection life. Baptism symbolises the death and burial of our old self. We can therefore praise God even when we pass through trials and testing because we know that it is through suffering that God prepares us to share in Jesus' glory, and as we die to self, Jesus' life will be more powerfully demonstrated through us.

Day 29

A Little is More than Enough

"There is a lad here who has five barley loaves and two fish, but what are these for so many people?" ... Jesus then took the loaves, and having given thanks, He distributed to those who were seated; likewise also of the fish as much as they wanted. ... So they gathered them up, and filled twelve baskets with fragments from the five barley loaves which were left over by those who had eaten. John 6:9,11,13

The above-quoted verses are taken from the miraculous and well-known story of the Feeding of the Five Thousand. I have heard messages in which the teacher has denied the miraculous aspect of this story and has tried to explain a natural way in which this multiplication of food could have happened. However, I have personally seen a miraculous multiplication of insufficient resources on several occasions when two key New Testament principles were obeyed. When we obey God's principles, even a little can be more than enough!

We will look briefly at these two principles. First, while Andrew dismissed this very sacrificial gift as being insufficient, Jesus thanked God for what they had even although it was not enough. It is essential that we learn the importance of gratitude and contentment even when we only have a little. We are so often like Andrew: whatever we have is not enough and this would include life-skills as well as finances and possessions. We undermine ourselves and our abilities, and moan and complain because we do not have as much as other people. How would you feel as a parent if, whenever you give a gift to your child, they only complain that it is not enough? Would you give them anything else?

Second, even although there was not enough food for the crowd, Jesus told the disciples to distribute it and there were twelve baskets left over. There is a biblical principle that we will receive in the same measure that we first give. If we give a little, we will only receive a little. In contrast, when we give generously – even if we only have a little – we will receive a generous amount. We can praise God even when we only have a little because, when we thank Him for what we have and share it with others, it will be more than enough.

Day 30

I will give You Rest

*"Come to Me, all who are weary and
heavy-laden, and I will give you rest."*
Matthew 11:28

An African church leader who I respect greatly has an interesting conversion testimony: he had been a member of a Marxist teenage gang who had gone into a Christian crusade in order to destroy it. They had filled their pockets with bottles and stones and were waiting for their leader to signal for them to act. The preacher used this passage as the text for his message. After his message, their leader was the first to go forward for prayer. They all followed him and were gloriously converted. My colleague commented that this text was very relevant as they were all heavy laden with bottles and stones!

The truth is that most of us are weary and burdened. Living in a fallen world can be painful, stressful, dangerous, tiring, and at times frustrating. Even as a Christian, we can face all the same difficulties with the added pressure of trying to share our faith with others and – in many countries – face severe opposition and persecution. Jesus even warned us that we would face trouble in this world, and so how can He also promise to give us rest.

Jesus is not promising that we will never face hardship or danger. He is promising that we can remain at peace even in the middle of a storm because His very powerful presence is with us. He demonstrated this peace when He and His disciples were in a boat when a storm arose. Despite the storm, Jesus was asleep, so the disciples woke him, fearing for their lives. He questioned their lack of faith and when He rebuked the wind, the storm subsided. He remained at peace because He trusted in His Father's sovereign presence.

We will become stressed and anxious if we carry the burden of life alone. Without God, we have very limited strength, abilities and resources with which to protect ourselves. We will remain at peace when we trust in His sovereign presence, His promised care, and His unlimited resources and power which will enable us to cope with any and every situation.

Day 31

My Burden is Light

*"Take My yoke upon you and learn from
Me, for I am gentle and humble in heart,
and YOU WILL FIND REST FOR YOUR SOULS.
For My yoke is easy and My burden is
light."* Matthew 11:29-30

Today, we will consider two more verses from this invitation of Jesus. First, let us think about the context in which these words were spoken. At the beginning of this chapter, Matthew tells us that Jesus was instructing his twelve disciples but then went to teach and to preach in the towns of Galilee. Immediately following this invitation, we are told that Jesus' disciples were picking some ears of corn and eating them when the Pharisees challenged them for not keeping the Sabbath. It would therefore appear that Jesus was speaking to a large crowd of people, and so we cannot exclude ourselves from this invitation. It is given to all of us, not just to an exclusive few.

The symbolism of being yoked to Jesus is easy for us to understand. It is most likely that He was referring to two oxen being yoked together in order to pull a cart. Another example would be two horses being yoked together in order to pull a carriage. Jesus, I believe, is emphasising the truth that God may give us loads which we cannot carry without His help. If we are struggling with a situation, it is just possible that we are trying to carry it alone.

Jesus is promising that when we walk together with Him, the burden that He gives us will be light. This has been my experience. I have seen many amazing miracles which include the provision and multiplication of resources, the planting of churches, and the opening of doors into unexpected and very fruitful ministries, to mention just a few. In every case, my role was very small and very easy and there was absolutely no way that I could take any credit for what happened. In direct contrast, I have also struggled and strived to produce fruit without seeing any positive results. The difference between the two could not be more extreme. When we walk closely with Jesus and follow His instructions, obedience is easy and the results glorious. Let us remember John the Baptist's words: He must become greater and I must become less.

Day 32

A Double Portion

*Instead of your shame you will have a
double portion, and instead of
humiliation they will shout for joy over
their portion. Therefore they will possess
a double portion in their land,
Everlasting joy will be theirs.* Isaiah 61:7

In this chapter, Isaiah is foreseeing a time when Israel will arise out of her sin and shine with God's glory. It would appear therefore that the promise in this verse is written specifically to those whose have faced shame and disgrace as a result of continued disobedience and idolatry, but there are also examples of, and promises for, restoration for those who have been shamed by the abusive behaviour of others and those who have faced loss through trials and testing.

The three phrases in this verse indicate that there are three areas where God is promising to bless us: first, restoring us to a place of honour. Second, restoring our spiritual inheritance. Third, restoring our earthly possessions. Whatever the cause of our shame, I believe that God is promising to restore what we have lost and raise us to a position where His glory shines upon us when we come back to Him. Jesus also confirms that God will compensate us for any current hardship and suffering. In His Sermon on the Mount, He promises that those who hunger will be satisfied, those who weep will laugh, and those who are hated, excluded and insulted will receive a great reward.

Let us consider two examples of the fulfilment of this promise: Job lost his family, his possessions and his livestock, his body was covered with boils, and he faced criticism from his three friends. However, after this period of trial, we read: *The LORD restored the fortunes of Job when he prayed for his friends, and the LORD increased all that Job had twofold.* (Job 42:10) God also vindicated him in front of his friends.

In the parable of the Prodigal Son, this son's behaviour was extremely selfish and offensive and yet, when he came to his senses, returned home, and sought forgiveness from his father, his father – who symbolises God – forgave him and restored him to his position of privilege and wealth within the family.

Day 33
Never Failing Compassion

The LORD'S lovingkindnesses indeed never
cease, For His compassions never fail.
They are new every morning; Great is
Your faithfulness. Lamentations 3:22-23

This whole chapter teaches us the importance of choosing to praise God even in very difficult situations. It also shows us the very human side of Jeremiah. This should encourage all of us, especially when negative emotions seek to overwhelm us. Verses 1-18 of this chapter are likely to surprise us. Jeremiah is clearly in utmost despair and he is blaming God for all the trouble that he is facing. Have you ever felt like that? I certainly have! The question that we need to ask ourselves is this: did God know how Jeremiah felt? Does He know how you feel? Of course, He does. Do you think that Jeremiah's outburst ruined his relationship with God? Clearly not! Sometimes honesty in relationships is essential. However, Jeremiah did not stay in that place and neither should we.

Starting in verse 19, Jeremiah challenges his thoughts and reminds himself of the truth: God's faithfulness, compassion and unfailing love never ceases or fails. He appears to be exhorting himself to continue to trust in the truth about God, even when circumstances appear to contradict that truth. When we pass through trials, we are not able to see the whole picture. However, as we read stories of biblical characters, we find that God is always faithful. Yesterday, we considered Job. He passed through a time of extreme trial and yet God restored a double portion of everything that he lost.

Joseph also passed through an extended period of extreme hardship and suffering. He was thrown into a pit and sold as a slave by his brothers. He was unjustly accused of rape by his master's wife and thrown into prison. Two fellow prisoners forgot to help him. But, during this very difficult time, God was preparing him for a position as second highest in the land, and He vindicated him in front of his brothers. Even although circumstances had appeared to deny the goodness and faithfulness of God, God proved Himself faithful to Joseph and Job. He will be faithful to us too if we continue to trust Him.

Day 34

Guaranteed Inheritance

*...when you believed, you were marked in
him with a seal, the promised Holy Spirit,
who is a deposit guaranteeing our
inheritance until the redemption of those
who are God's possession – to the praise
of his glory.* Ephesians 1:13b-14 (NIV)

Many of us would like to know what the future holds. Life, however, is unpredictable. We all know that despite our very best efforts to plan for our future, there is the continual possibility of unplanned disasters such as serious illnesses, job losses or natural disasters. All these uncertainties and even the mention of the word cancer or dementia can cause us anxiety. No one can be sure what our future on earth will be. One thing, however, of which we can be certain, is our eternal future. The above-quoted verses tell us that God has even provided evidence of our destiny so that we can remain at peace.

There are four words in these verses to consider: the first word is 'seal'. A seal is rarely used in our modern society, but it was used extensively in the past. Any person with wealth or a title would wear a signet ring with his own special design and initials embossed on it. When writing a letter or signing a document, a small blob of melted wax would be poured onto the page and then stamped with the signet ring to prove the authenticity of the document. God has sealed us with the Holy Spirit guaranteeing our sonship and future inheritance.

The second word is 'deposit'. If we purchase an expensive object, we are often required to pay a deposit as proof of our desire to buy the object and evidence that we will pay the rest of the sum required. In a similar way, God has given us the Holy Spirit as current evidence that He has paid the full price for our redemption and that our future is secure. The third word 'guaranteeing' is a strong word which further emphasises the security of our future. The fourth word 'inheritance' refers to other verses which tell us that we are a joint heir with Christ: our future inheritance is therefore the same as His. When we are tempted to doubt our salvation, the presence of the Holy Spirit within us, proves beyond any doubt both our current and future position in Christ.

Day 35
Bonds of Love

When Israel was a youth I loved him, And
out of Egypt I called My son. ... I led them
with cords of a man, with bonds of love,
And I became to them as one who lifts the
yoke from their jaws; And I bent down
and fed them. Hosea 11:1,4

As we read through this chapter, we hear a cry of love from God's heart towards His children, Israel, and of the grief that they have caused Him through their rebellion and disobedience. He has poured love and care into their lives, but they have rejected it. Surely, we would not expect God to expose His emotions to the very people who have spurned Him. Furthermore, He has not abandoned them, but is appealing to them to come back to Him.

Although this is an Old Testament passage, the love expressed in it also applies to us as new covenant believers. Many New Testament passages tell us that God has adopted us as His children and that He will go to any length to find us and to draw us back to Himself regardless of the depth of sin to which we have fallen. There is no one who is beyond the reach of His love and mercy.

God led them with bonds of love. Let us meditate on these words: first, the word 'led' tells us that God goes ahead of us, preparing the way for our feet and ensuring that the path is safe. Second, He leads us. He does not leave us alone to work out the route for ourselves. He knows the best path that is not beyond our ability or stamina. Third, He is leading us to a better place. He accepts us as we are, surrounded by the consequences of our sin, but He wants to lead us to a better place of peace, abundance and joy. Fourth, He leads us with human kindness, He does not drive us harshly from behind with a stick as we do with cows and goats but draws us forward with love.

God also describes how He lifted the yoke from their jaws. His desire is to set us free from everything that would seek to control us, crush us or to hinder our progress. He also speaks of how He bent down to feed them. He provides us with the nourishment which we need, not from an elevated and distant position above us, but He bends down in humility to our level beside us.

Day 36

God's Word Hold Us Up

*Peter said to Him, "Lord, if it is You,
command me to come to You on the
water." And He said, "Come!" And Peter got
out of the boat, and walked on the water
and came toward Jesus.*
Matthew 14:28-29

It is my strong belief that if we want to see God's miraculous power flowing through our lives, we need to be out of our depth. We need to live in a place where we cannot live without Him. One example of this is the disciples. They not only left their families but also their means of earning an income. The moment that they responded to Jesus' call they were all out of their depth.

This New Testament story of Peter stepping out of the boat and walking on water describes this process well. There are at least eight lessons which we can learn from this story. First, Peter asked Jesus to command him to come. He had come to understand the power of Jesus' words and knew that he could only walk on the water if Jesus told him to do so. Second, Peter obeyed Jesus' word to him even although obedience would have seemed impossible.

Third, Jesus' one word "Come" was enough. There was nothing else which held him on top of the waves. When God gives us His word, He may not immediately provide other resources which would make our obedience any easier. Jesus' word did not calm the waves. Fourth, Peter was safer walking on the water than the disciples were in the boat. If a storm had arisen, Jesus' word would have held Peter above the waves, but the boat may have sunk.

Sixth, Peter had to get out of the boat before he saw the miracle. God does not perform a miracle until after we have stepped out in faith. Let us remember the occasions when Jesus told a sick person to perform some act of obedience before they received their healing. Seventh, when we are out of our depth, we are no longer dependent on our own limited resources and all the unlimited resources of God will be made available to us. Eighth, when we are out of the boat, we will see a constant demonstration of God's presence which will build a deep security in our hearts which cannot be shaken by any storm. Let us thank God that when He speaks a Word to us, it will never fail to support us.

Day 37

The Lord's Glory

Arise, shine; for your light has come, And the glory of the LORD has risen upon you. For behold, darkness will cover the earth and deep darkness the peoples; But the LORD will rise upon you And His glory will appear upon you. Nations will come to your light, And kings to the brightness of your rising. Isaiah 60:1-3

In this chapter, God is speaking through Isaiah about the future glories of Israel and it includes promises of many blessings including wealth and joy, and with those who have despised us bowing down at our feet. This theme is continued in both the Old and New Testaments: the many blessings which will follow submission and obedience to Him. In an earlier meditation, we considered the choice which God presented to Israel: the choice between life and death, and blessings and curses. Each one of us has this same choice. We can choose what kind of life we want to life. We can also choose what our future destiny will be.

In these three verses, God is promising that His glory will appear over us and that kings and nations will be drawn towards that light. This, I believe, will be true for those of us who draw close to God; to those of us who spend time in His presence. This principle is not only spiritually true, but it is also naturally true as well. We are all effected by our surroundings. If we spend time with people who are loving, kind and joyful, we will be uplifted by their presence. In direct contrast, if we spend time with those who are angry, critical and miserable, this will have a very negative effect on our emotional well-being. If we spend time with God, the brightness of His glory will radiate from us.

Let us consider two biblical characters who shone with God's glory. First, we read in Exodus, chapter 34, that whenever Moses spoke with the Lord, his face was radiant, and the Israelites were afraid to come near him. Whenever he came out from God's presence, he therefore covered his face with a veil. Second, in the books of Acts, chapter 6, we read that when Stephen was seized and brought before the Sanhedrin, his face was like the face of an angel. Later, when he was stoned to death, he looked up to heaven and saw the glory of God.

Day 38

Holy and Blameless

...just as He chose us in Him before the foundation of the world, that we would be holy and blameless before Him...
Ephesians 1:4

Most of us will have had to take an examination to test our abilities at some time in our lives. It is most likely to have been at school, but it could also be at university or in order to be accepted for a job or for some training course. The pass mark will vary from situation to situation. Sometimes it will to be as low as getting 50% of the answers correct, but it is often higher. However, we will never be expected to get 100% of our examination paper correct.

God's requirements are different, and His standards are very high. He requires 100% perfection, which is a standard which none of us can reach. This is the reason why none of us can earn our salvation. It is impossible for us to reach the standard which God requires. His requirements are so high that it was necessary for Him to complete the standard for us. This is what Jesus achieved for us. He lived a perfect life and gives us all the credit for His perfection.

I remember one passage in the biography of St. Thérèse of Lisieux in which she describes so profoundly the wonderful way that Jesus transforms and perfects our lives. She was thinking about the pathway to perfection and concluded that there was no way in which she could achieve perfection through her own efforts but wrote that she was not in any way downcast. She described how she saw the pathway to perfection like a staircase, and that she was sitting at the bottom looking up at it when Jesus came down from the top and, picking her up in His arms, carried her to the very top.

Let us therefore ask ourselves one important question. How do we see ourselves? We will probably give a list of our faults and weaknesses. This is NOT how God sees those of us who have put our faith in Jesus. God sees us as holy and blameless. This is NOT a promise for the future. It is how He sees us NOW because of all that Jesus have achieved for us through His life and death. Jesus has fulfilled God's high standard of perfection for us.

Day 39
The 'Divine Exchange'

For you know the grace of our Lord Jesus
Christ, that though He was rich, yet for
your sake He became poor, so that you
through His poverty might become rich.
2 Corinthians 8:9

We considered yesterday how we are holy and blameless in God's sight but emphasised that this is not through any good works for which we can take any credit. No. It is through what is often called the 'divine exchange', in which Jesus takes upon Himself our sin and God credits us with Jesus' perfection.

This 'divine exchange' was the transaction achieved for us through the death of Jesus on the cross and it is a gift of grace that God gives to all of us who put and faith in Christ Jesus. This transaction was achieved entirely by God on our behalf and cannot be earned or deserved, it can only be received by faith. Furthermore, it is offered to everyone equally regardless of our wealth, status, age, parentage, nationality or the depth of our depravity and sin.

To better understand this expression: divine exchange, let us consider what happened when Jesus went to the cross. Jesus, who is perfect in every way, took upon Himself the sin of everyone of us. Although He was perfect, He became sin! Every sin which we have ever committed or will commit in the future was laid upon His shoulders to carry to the cross. He has taken the full punishment for the sin of every one of us so that we are now free. Amazing though this is, this is not all that God achieved for us through Jesus' death. Jesus not only took our sin but, in exchange, He gives us His righteousness.

The above verses describe this exchange further. Jesus, who was rich, took our poverty and in return gives us His riches. The words 'poverty' and 'riches' have a greater meaning than just money. They refer to all the spiritual resources and benefits enjoyed by Jesus. This is the exchange: Jesus takes our sin and poverty and gives us His righteousness and riches. We can also describe this exchange in a different way: God's mercy means that we do not receive the punishment that we do deserve. God's grace means that we receive all the blessings and benefits that we do not deserve. How amazing is that?

Day 40
Partakers

*For by these He has granted to us His
precious and magnificent promises, so
that by them you may become partakers
of the divine nature, having escaped the
corruption that is in the world by lust.*
2 Peter 1:4

Jesus warned us that we would face trouble in this world. Certainly, I have found that placing our faith in Jesus does not lead to an easy stress-free life. Quite the opposite! In fact, life often becomes even more testing and stressful as we mature. I regularly find myself in situations where it is very difficult to respond in a godly way. It is not only a matter of resisting our own selfish desires, but it is also offering love and grace to those who use and abuse us.

We considered in an earlier meditation how God's standards are very high. God not only requires us to forgive all those who mistreat us, but Jesus tells us to bless them as well. This is contrary to our fallen human nature which does not instantly change when we receive salvation. Our natural desire for justice and revenge can be very strong. Forgiving those who mistreat us once can be difficult, but continual abuse can be very difficult to deal with as God requires.

It is for this reason that Peter tells us that God gives us His very great and precious promises. We very often look at God's promises in order to believe for healing or provision of some kind. However, this is not the reason which Peter gives in the above-quoted verse. Peter tells us that God gives us His promises so that we can participate in His divine nature. It is through faith in His promises that we are enabled to resist behaving according to our fallen human nature and instead behave according to His divine character.

I am currently facing some extremely difficult and stressful circumstances. When I prayed about it, God likened my situation to Peter getting out of the boat. Peter could not walk on the water without God's supernatural power to hold him up. Similarly, He is allowing me to face circumstances where I am out of my depth and cannot respond well without His promised help. Where God sets high standards, He also provides the means for us to obey them.

Day 41

No Condemnation

> Therefore, there is now no
> condemnation for those who are in
> Christ Jesus... Who will bring any
> charge against those whom God has
> chosen? It is God who justifies. Who
> then is the one who condemns? No
> one... Romans 8:1, 33-34a (NIV)

In the Book of Revelation, chapter 12, we read that our accuser (Satan), who makes accusations against us before God day and night, has been thrown down. Satan's downfall is, of course, still in the future. At present, he is still very much alive and very actively accusing us. One reason why his accusations are so relentless is because he knows that it is sin (submission and obedience to him instead of to God) which gives him access into our lives and power over us. It is through accusation that he seeks to hold onto his control of us.

It is therefore extremely important that we resist the temptation to listen to Satan's lies and allow him to condemn us. Once we allow him to deceive us in this way, we lose our freedom and he regains control. This deception is very subtle, and we need to be alert to his schemes. It can appear to be a sign of humility to confess that we are sinners, but it is really a lack of faith in the cleansing power of the blood of Jesus that was shed so sacrificially for us and it will rob us of the wonderful freedom that Jesus paid such a high price to give us. If we sin, we need to repent and ask God to forgive us in order to remain free, but we must not allow Satan to bring general condemnation into our lives.

In the above-quoted verses, Paul asks the question: who will bring a charge against us when God has chosen us and justified us. There is no higher authority than God Himself. In a court of law on earth, it is sometimes possible to appeal against a judge and jury's decision and to take a case to a higher court with even greater authority, hoping for a different verdict. However, if God has pronounced us innocent, there is no higher authority who is able to reverse this pronouncement.

As Paul writes: who is the one who can condemn us. No one! Our case has already been taken to this highest authority possible and we have been pronounced innocent and free from condemnation.

Day 42

Incomparable Riches

...in order that in the coming ages he might show the incomparable riches of his grace, expressed in his kindness to us in Christ Jesus. Ephesians: 2:7 (NIV)

This above-quoted verse is just one verse in a long paragraph in which Paul describes some of the many blessings which we receive in Christ. Paul begins this paragraph by describing the depths of sin and depravity to which we had fallen before going on to consider the mercy and grace that God has lavished upon us. The contrast between our fallen state and very blessed state to which God has lifted us, emphasises the extreme nature of His mercy and grace.

In this verse, Paul gives one reason why God has chosen to pour His many blessings into our lives: He wants the world to be able to see a demonstration of the incomparable riches of His grace, and He has chosen us to demonstrate this through pouring His kindness into our lives. God has chosen us to display His goodness to the world. We need, therefore, to ask ourselves this question: when people look at us, do they see any evidence of God's grace and kindness?

In order to answer this important question, let us ask ourselves some more questions: have we received by faith the many benefits and blessings which God has promised us? How often do we tell others how God has transformed and enriched our lives? Do we take every opportunity to give testimony of how He blesses us each day? Do our faces display joy and fulfilment? Do we give generously, sharing the blessings which we have received with others? Do our lives demonstrate the power of the Holy Spirit within us? Do we demonstrate love to others in the same way as God has demonstrated His love to us?

In direct contrast, do we moan and complain when we face trials and testing? Do we regularly tell others about all the hardships which we face? Do we hold onto our finances and possessions because we do not trust God to meet our needs? Do we expect others to solve our problems for us? Do our faces look downcast and anxious? In order to achieve His goal: God will pour His richest blessing into the lives of those who display and share them with others.

Day 43
Good News

*'The Spirit of the Lord is on me, because
he has anointed me to proclaim good
news to the poor. He has sent me to
proclaim freedom for the prisoners and
recovery of sight for the blind, to set the
oppressed free..."* Luke 4:18 (NIV)

These words are part of a prophesy about the Messiah given by Isaiah. They were read out in the synagogue by Jesus who also confirmed that this prophesy was speaking about Him. The passage in Isaiah 61, is longer than that quoted by Luke and is referred to as Jesus' manifesto. The whole passage, of which the above verse is just a part, describes Jesus' mission on earth.

This verse lists four groups of people whose lives Jesus came to completely and radically transform. This is very good news for the poor, the prisoner, the blind and the oppressed. God, of course, loves every one of us equally. However, it is those of us who recognise our sinfulness or who face trouble or hardship, who are most open to see their need of a saviour.

Let us consider briefly how Jesus can transform the lives of these four different groups. First, when the

Bible refers to the poor, it does not exclusively mean those who are in financial need, for its meaning is much broader. Jesus spoke about the poor in spirit, referring to all those who recognise that they have a need, to those who are not proud, independent and self-reliant.

Second, the word 'prisoner' is not referring to incarceration within prison walls but being held captive in the mind through addictions or the consequences of emotional abuse. Jesus gives us peace and freedom in our mind regardless of our circumstances. Third, the word 'blind' refers to those who are physical or spiritually blind. He healed many who were physically blind, but He also opens our eyes to see and understand spiritual truth, enabling us to see, believe and receive all the promised blessings. Finally, He helps those who are oppressed in the mind by spiritual forces and those oppressed by the dominance and abuse of others. The indwelling Holy Spirit gives us the power and authority to be an overcomer in every situation.

Day 44

Alive with Christ

*When you were dead in your transgressions
and the uncircumcision of your flesh, He made
you alive together with Him, having forgiven
us all our transgressions, having canceled out
the certificate of debt consisting of decrees
against us, which was hostile to us; and He
has taken it out of the way, having nailed it to
the cross.* Colossians 2:13-14

Paul begins this passage by describing our position without Christ: we were dead in our sin, and our flesh was alive and in control. We may have considered ourselves to be alive, independent and free but this was not our true position. We need to face up to the truth: no person without Christ is free. We may have thought that we were able to make our own independent decisions, but we were controlled by the world, the flesh and the devil. It is only when we make Jesus our Lord and Saviour, that we are set free from their control.

God has made us alive by forgiving our sin and cancelling all legal charges against us. We all recognise that if we owe someone a sum of money, we are not free until that debt is paid. Any person who is in debt is under the control of the person to whom they owe money. This is the position that we were in. Our sin was a debt which gave Satan control over us, and he used the world and our flesh to control us and thus to keep us subservient to him. We were just like a puppet being controlled by the strings held by the puppet master.

Our sin condemned us. It is as if we were hand-cuffed and standing in the dock in a court of law, guarded by police, and not able to escape the appropriate punishment for our crime. We were not able to pay our enormous debt and therefore could not free ourselves. It is only because God paid our debt for us that we are now free. Paul tells us that Jesus took the list of charges made against us and nailed them to the cross. However, our continued freedom is dependent upon our obedience to God. Our choice is a simple one: we can choose to obey God and to remain free, or we can continue in our rebellion against Him and thus to be controlled by the world, the flesh and the devil. God has taken our punishment upon Himself and paid our debt in full. Let us choose to walk in that freedom and to enjoy all the benefits which Jesus gained for us.

Day 45

God commands a Blessing

*Behold, how good and how pleasant it is
for brothers to dwell together in unity! ...
For there the LORD commanded the
blessing - life forever.* Psalm 133:1,3b

I have learned through many personal experiences how important it is that we work in unity with fellow believers. We will consider three passages in the Bible which show why it is so important. The psalmist's words, quoted above, tells us that it is when we live in unity, that God commands a blessing. We have seen evidence of this in Malawi: one month before the harvest was due this year, the rain stopped in one district and crops were starting to die. I suggested that pastors from areas where the rains continued to be good, travel to this area to stand in unity with their brethren and to pray for a blessing of rain. On their journey home it started to rain and rained continuously for five days.

Second, the gospels of Matthew, Mark and Luke all include Jesus' warning that a kingdom divided against itself cannot stand. God showed me that when we fail to live in unity, we become vulnerable to spiritual attack. He reminded me that crocodiles rarely attack large groups of people and so when believers in Africa are baptised in a river, they are safe. Women collecting water, however, are often attacked and killed. He showed me that demonic forces are like crocodiles, and that we are vulnerable to attack when we are divided by unforgiveness, slander, gossip and criticism. I saw another demonstration of the importance of unity when a Christian friend travelled to Albania. Upon his return, he experienced regular dark nightmares. However, after a group of us stood united, and identified with him in prayer, these nightmares stopped.

Third, in the second and fourth chapters of Acts, we read that all the believers shared everything in common, selling property and possessions in order to help those in need and that the Lord added daily those who were being saved and many wonders and signs were being performed by the apostles. This would support the psalmist's words: that where there is love and unity between believers, God's presence, blessing and power is demonstrated.

Day 46

Kept from Stumbling

*To him who is able to keep you from
stumbling and to present you before his
glorious presence without fault and with
great joy...* Jude 1:24 (NIV)

I have just moved into a new house and have had
some extensive work done in the garden. Now that
the work is finished, the paving is perfectly level and
devoid of all trip-hazards. However, the old paving
had been loose and uneven, and during the work, the
area had been muddy and covered with piles of earth
as well as lower areas which had been dug for the
foundations of the new paving. Great care was
therefore needed when walking across it. This muddy
and uneven landscape is a good picture of life. It is full
of hazards of many different kinds, and if we are not
careful, we can fall and hurt ourselves.

Jesus never promised us that life would be easy, but
He does promise to walk with us and to keep us from
stumbling. A good example of this is when Jesus held
out his hand to lift Peter when he looked down at the
waves and started to sink. If you are walking hand in
hand with someone, even if you do trip, you will not

fall far. In my garden, the trip-hazards were visible. In life, we cannot always see the dangers until it is too late. It is far better to walk with someone who can see the dangers ahead and warn us about them so that we avoid them.

A good example would be the very dangerous job of clearing a mine field where it is necessary to use equipment which can detect where the mines have been laid so that they can be approached with great care. In the same way, Jesus is able to detect where danger lies and show us how to avoid hurting ourselves.

Jude tells us that Jesus will present us before God's glorious presence. This is a wonderful and comforting truth. When our time comes to depart this life, we will not be alone for Jesus will meet us and lead us into God's presence. I have attended very grand events where each guest is introduced by title and name. I imagine that this is how it will be. Jesus will introduce us to the heavenly court, giving our name and confirming our God-given righteousness without which we would have no right to be there. What a joy-filled event this will be.

Day 47
All Things!

He who did not spare His own Son, but delivered Him over for us all, how will He not also with Him freely give us all things? Romans 8:32

Most parents will go to any length, and pay any price, to protect their children. I have seen TV dramas in which a parent has falsely confessed to murder because they believe that their child has committed this crime. They have been prepared to suffer the consequences themselves for a crime that they did not commit in order to prevent their child suffering. These dramas have been fictitious, but I believe that they indicate the price that parents will pay in order to protect their children. It was therefore extremely costly for God to give up His own Son and to watch Him suffer such extreme agony on a cross.

True love can cause considerable pain. When we love someone, it will cause us untold pain to watch them suffering. God is love. It must, therefore, cause Him intense pain to watch all the suffering in the world: suffering inflicted by cruelty, suffering caused by war and natural disasters, suffering from rejection, anxiety and depression, suffering caused by verbal and physical abuse, and suffering due to famine and hunger. I know the pain that it causes me, as a fallen human being, when I see a child, adult or animal be cruelly treated. How much more must it cause God pain to witness so much pain throughout the world on a continual basis. God loves us so much that He gave up His own Son to extreme suffering because it was the only way to rescue us.

Paul goes on to draw the natural conclusion: if God loves us so much that He is prepared to give up His own Son for us, will He not also give us everything that we need to live life to the full. He is not, of course, suggesting that God will give us everything that we want, especially if we want things that will cause us harm. A desire for more possessions, larger houses, expensive status-symbol cars, or excessive food and alcohol will not give us joy and peace. In direct contrast, they can lead us on a path to self-destruction. He will, however, provide everything which we need for an abundant and fruitful life.

Day 48

Everything We Need

...seeing that His divine power has granted to us everything pertaining to life and godliness, through the true knowledge of Him who called us by His own glory and excellence. 2 Peter 1:3

We have already considered how God's required standards are very high. He is perfect in every way and this is the standard that He sets for us. Please imagine that you, as an ordinary and not very wealthy citizen, have been sent an invitation to attend a banquet held in the king's palace. Would you arrive at this banquet dressed in dirty and ragged clothing? Surely, you would make every effort to buy or to borrow a suitable outfit for such an occasion.

Jesus told a parable in Matthew's gospel, chapter 22, about a wedding banquet. He described how many refused the invitation to attend this banquet and so the host sent his servants out into the streets to gather as many people as possible so that the hall would be full. However, when the host came in to see the guests, he noticed a man who was not wearing suitable clothing, so he told his servants to tie him hand and foot and throw him outside into the darkness.

This parable may seem harsh. The description of the treatment given to this man is often left out of the story, and we just concentrate on that fact that everyone is invited to the banquet. However, the truth is that although the kingdom of heaven is open to everyone, however great our past sins and failures, God requires us to 'wear suitable clothing' (for us to live a godly life).

Fortunately, God does not expect us to live perfect lives without help. Peter uses the past tense and tells us that God has given us everything that we need to live a godly life. We already have everything that we need: we do not need to earn it or even to pray for it. We only need to believe it, to receive it by faith, and to choose to change how we behave.

In Ephesians 4, Paul tells us to put off our old self and to put on the new righteous and holy self. In Colossians 3, he writes that we have taken off our old self and have put on the new self. Both passages describe this change like putting on new clothing. We simply choose to take off one garment and to put on another.

Day 49

His Great Love

*But God, being rich in mercy, because of
His great love with which He loved us,
even when we were dead in our
transgressions, made us alive together
with Christ (by grace you have been
saved)...* Ephesians 2:4-5

We will consider three important truths in these two verses. First, it is because He loves us so much that God was willing to pay the highest price imaginable in order to redeem us from a place of death: the sacrifice of His one and only Son. Sometimes, we are prepared to pay a high price for something, but we often have a selfish and ulterior motive. We give because we want to receive something back. In direct contrast, God's only motive was love, and the consequent desire to do everything possible for our well-being and happiness.

Second, we need to recognise the seriousness of our past condition: we were dead. We were not yet dead physically – although it would only have been a matter of time before our physical body would both die and decay – but we were dead spiritually. Our sin had resulted in our spiritual death and complete separation from God with no possible way that we could, through our own efforts, redeem ourselves. The Old Testament teaches us that only a perfect and spotless lamb could pay the required price for sin, and this sacrifice was only a temporary solution. Thousands of lambs had to be slaughtered year after year until the blood of Jesus paid a full and permanent price for our sin. The important point to remember here is that because we have all sinned and are therefore imperfect, we cannot purchase our own redemption.

Third, it is therefore by God's grace alone that we have been redeemed. We can never earn it or deserve it. We were completely helpless and unable to pay the necessary price for salvation. This is the point that Jesus emphasised in His parable of the 'Unmerciful Servant' in Matthew 18. The servant's debt was so large that he was unable to pay it back. Only the triune God is perfect, only He can therefore take the necessary punishment for our sin. We cannot take any credit for the very blessed position to which God has restored us. We can only thank and praise Him for His unparalleled love, mercy and grace.

Day 50
The Oil of Joy

*"The Spirit of the Lord God is upon me,
because the Lord has anointed and
qualified me to... To grant [consolation
and joy] to those who mourn in Zion—to
give them an ornament (a garland or
diadem) of beauty instead of ashes, the
oil of joy instead of mourning, the
garment [expressive] of praise instead of
a heavy, burdened, and failing spirit..."*
Isaiah 61:1a, 3a (AMP)

This passage is part of a prophesy which describes Jesus' mission through His life, death and resurrected position in heaven. He came to earth and chose to die in order to rescue us and to lift us from the dire place to which we had fallen. We will focus on the three blessings promised in this passage, but first let us notice that the phrases 'to grant' and 'to give' applies to all three. When we find ourselves grieving over the death of a loved one or facing events which lead us to despair, God promises to lift us and to comfort us. We do not overcome through striving and self-effort, but through turning to Him for help.

First, to grant consolation and joy to those who

mourn in Zion, giving them an ornament of beauty instead of ashes. When we grieve over the loss of a loved one and we feel as if we have lost a sense of purpose or that our life is reduced to ashes, God promises to restore our joy by providing us with a source of comfort and encouragement, giving us a new goal and sense of purpose.

Second, to give us the oil of joy instead of mourning. In the Bible, oil is associated with anointing, and this is not something that we can provide for ourselves. It is a gift from God. In Psalm 133, the psalmist describes a precious oil being poured upon our heads and coming down to the edge of our robes. When God anoints us with joy, it will lavishly cover our whole body.

Third, to give us a garment of praise instead of a heavy, burdened and failing spirit. As with each of these three promises, God promises to GIVE us the help that we need. If we look to Him when events tempt us to despair, He will pour thoughts, words or songs of praise into our hearts, enabling us to focus on Him and to remain positive and full of faith in the most negative situations.

Day 51
Oaks of Righteousness

...To grant those who mourn in Zion ... So they will be called oaks of righteousness, The planting of the LORD, that He may be glorified. Isaiah 61:3a, c (NIV)

The above-quoted passage is a continuation of the prophesy describing Jesus' mission which we considered yesterday. Today, I would like to consider five encouraging truths that we can learn from this brief passage. First, let us focus again on the phrase 'to grant'. We do not overcome through striving and self-effort, but through turning to God so that He can GIVE us the help that we need.

The second, third and fourth truths all focus on the symbolism of the oak tree. Let us consider the size and seemingly insignificance of an acorn. It may appear small and insignificant but when it is planted in the ground, it will grow into a huge and very strong oak tree, much larger and the wood more valuable than most trees. The second encouragement is therefore that God chooses small, weak and insignificant people who are prepared to lay down their lives and to die to themselves – symbolised in baptism by being buried under the water – and third, He transforms them into significant, strong and fruitful channels of His love, grace and power. However small and insignificant we are in ourselves; God will transform us into something great and magnificent.

Fourth, the strength and value of an oak tree depends on where it is grown. An oak tree which is planted in a colder climate such as the UK, grows into a valuable 'hard wood' which can be used to produce strong and very valuable furniture. However, I have been told that there are oak trees in South Africa, but they are only a soft wood. It is the long cold winters that slow down the growth of the tree, producing a more dense and valuable hard wood. Similarly, it is trials and testing which produces strength and character in our lives.

Fifth, when we allow God to transform our lives, we will bring glory to Him. In and of ourselves, this is impossible, but when we stop trying to produce fruit through our own plans and efforts, and instead look to Him for guidance and an infilling of His love, grace and miraculous power, He will be glorified.

Day 52

Predestined for Adoption

He predestined us to adoption as sons
through Jesus Christ to Himself,
according to the kind intention of His
will... Ephesians 1:5

The word 'predestined' describes an event, career, position or achievement which cannot be prevented or altered because it is determined by God. It is not something, therefore, that we can aspire to or achieve through our own efforts. The fact that God has predestined us to be adopted as His son or daughter is entirely determined and achieved through His love, grace and sovereign power, and there is no power which can prevent its fulfilment except for our own lack of faith in His goodness and submission to His plans.

All this is very good news! Despite the fact that we - as Christian believers - are caught up in a battle between good and evil, and will have experienced the opposition, hardship and suffering that is the very nature of any battle, we can be assured that there is no power which can prevent the fulfilment of God's plan for our life, a plan which was determined long before we were even born.

I recently watched a DVD of a film showing the Battle of Waterloo, which was fought on Sunday, 18th June 1815. This film, which must have used thousands of extras in its battle scenes, gives a graphic picture of the horror, suffering and carnage of battle. In direct contrast to those who have lived through the trauma of war, most of us who were born after 1945 in the UK have never experienced the horror of conflict and can therefore find it difficult to understand the nature of the spiritual battle of which we are a part, feeling confused, abandoned and forsaken by God when life is difficult.

Our adoption is in accordance with God's kind intention and will. He adopts us because this is His goal. He loves us and wants to restore us into His family where He can love and care for us. He loves us and wants to give us all the privileges and blessings of sonship. Jesus described the father-heart of God in His parable of The Prodigal Son. Regardless of the depth to which his son had fallen, the father's love for his son was not diminished, and when he returned to the family, he was completely restored to his former position of privilege.

Day 53

Predestined for His Glory

... also we have obtained an inheritance,
having been predestined according to His
purpose who works all things after the
counsel of His will, to the end that we
who were the first to hope in Christ
would be to the praise of His glory.
Ephesians 1:11-12

Just six verses after the verse which we considered yesterday, Paul repeats the same word 'predestined', emphasising once again that, as Christian believers, our destiny has been determined by God, Himself, and cannot be altered or changed. In verse 11, Paul refers to another benefit of sonship: we gain an inheritance. Let us notice that the past perfect tense has been used here. As the word 'inheritance' refers to benefits received after a person's death, I have mistakenly understood this to be a benefit that we receive in heaven. The truth, however, is that we receive an inheritance while we are still alive and so we have already been provided with an inheritance appropriate to sonship.

Paul goes on to give even more detail about the very

significant role that God plays in our lives, for He has not only prepared and planned for our rescue and redemption, but He also works out everything to conform with the plans which He has prepared for us. These words remind us of that although we are not able to see it, God is constantly working behind the scenes to prevent anything which cannot be used constructively to achieve His goals for us, and therefore testing, hardship and suffering are only allowed when they can have positive benefits for either our earthly and our eternal destiny.

In verse twelve, Paul describes God's final purpose for every one of us: that we might be for the praise of His glory. We were created to bring glory to God; not through our own efforts and achievements because it is not possible for us, as fallen and selfish human beings, to glorify our creator. We can only glorify Him by allowing His glory to flow through us. Just as the light shining from the moon is only the reflection of the rays from the sun, so our lives were created to reflect the light, grace, love and glory of God to a lost, dark and fallen world. The moon has no light of its own and nor do we! It is only able to light up the night sky by allowing the rays from the sun to be reflected from it surface.

Day 54
God's Workmanship

For we are His workmanship, created in
Christ Jesus for good works, which God
prepared beforehand so that we would
walk in them. Ephesians: 2:10

We are God's workmanship and we read in Genesis, chapter 1, that everything which God made is very good. God never makes a mistake or creates anything which is less than perfect. However, just as children play in the mud in their clean clothing, so we behave in a way which spoils our spotless perfection. But just as mud can be washed off, so even our most heinous sins can be cleansed by the blood of Jesus. Many of us may also bear the scars or suffer from physical defects as a result of living in a fallen world but these do not undermine our value or significance. Instead, therefore, of focusing on our weaknesses and failures, let us thank God that we are wonderfully made (Psalm 139:14).

Paul is also reminding us that we were created in Christ Jesus for good works. The key phrase here is 'in Christ Jesus': we can only do good works if we remain in Him. We considered yesterday, how the moon can only light up the night sky if it allows the sun's rays to reflect off its surface. This same truth can also be applied to our ability to do good works: we are enabled to do good works when we allow His love, grace and compassion to flow through us.

There are a few days each month when the moon is not visible because the earth blocks the sun's rays from falling on it, but there has never been a day when the sun's rays have not shone in its direction. In a similar way, God's love, grace and compassion never ceases from shining upon us. Just as clouds may block our ability to feel the warmth of the sun, so a variety of different factors may block a sense of God's love, presence and power, but that does not mean that He has paused - even for a moment – from shining upon us.

Let us, therefore, believe in God's constant love, allowing it to penetrate our hearts and lives, even when we do not feel it, and to share everything which we receive from Him with others. The more that we share the blessings which we receive and empty ourselves of 'self', the more God can fill us with Himself.

Day 55
Unforgettable

"Can a woman forget her nursing child and have no compassion on the son of her womb? Even these may forget, but I will not forget you. Behold, I have inscribed you on the palms of My hands; Your walls are continually before Me." Isaiah 49:15-16

In an earlier meditation we considered the caring and self-sacrificing love that God created within mothers – both human and animal. It is a compassion which is especially strong when their offspring are vulnerable and unable to care for themselves. During the gesticulation period, all human babies and most mammals are entirely dependent on their mothers and will not survive without her provision of milk. In some countries, the manufacture of bottled baby-milk has lessened a baby's dependence on its mother but in biblical times and in many other countries, this dependence remains unchanged.

This truth of a baby's dependence on its mother is a picture of how God created us to depend upon Him. Despite all our efforts to live independent lives, the truth is that we need God in just the same way as a very young baby needs its mother. In this prophesy from Isaiah, God is reassuring us of His constant care and compassion. He is encouraging us to look to Him for nurture by promising that He will never forget us. It is possible that this symbolism of a woman and nursing child is used to remind us of our need to depend on Him.

God uses further symbolism to emphasise that we are never out of His sight. The psalmist understood this truth and wrote:

> *Where can I go from Your Spirit? Or where can I flee from Your presence? If I ascend to heaven, You are there; if I make my bed in Sheol, behold, You are there. If I take the wings of the dawn, if I dwell in the remotest part of the sea, even there Your hand will lead me, And Your right hand will lay hold of me.*
> Psalm 139:7-10

Many parents have monitors so that they can see and hear their babies when they are asleep elsewhere in the house. This is a picture of how God cares for us. If human parents go to such lengths to care for their babies, how much more will God care for us. There is never a moment when He is not watching us.

Day 56

The Lord Will Take Me Up

For my father and my mother have
forsaken me, But the LORD will take me up.
Psalm 27:10

With the current breakdown within so many families, very large numbers of children are growing up without knowing the loving care of a father and a mother. Many grow up in one-parent families were that parent has struggled to provide and to care for their children. Other children have been physically and sexually abused by their parents. These situations can cause significant damage to any child which can last for their entire lives. God created us to be loved and nurtured by both a father and a mother who should be role-models, showing us and teaching us how to mature into responsible adults.

As a result, many of us will have lacked the love, security and discipline that we should have received. We may be struggling to survive and to function but lack the emotional stability and knowledge needed to live contented, happy and successful lives. Through no fault of our own, we find ourselves lacking the courage and discernment required to make good choices. Following past abuse, we can develop such a poor opinion of ourselves that we continue to allow others to abuse us and have no confidence in our ability to succeed. Therefore, despite our best efforts, we pass through one disaster after another.

Although it is not possible to undo the past, it is God's plan to take us up and to give us the parental care that we have lacked. He desires to heal our past hurts, to restore what we have lost, and to use our negative experiences for good. Let us remind ourselves of the story of Joseph. Despite his very hurtful experiences, God gave him his own family and restored his relationship with his own family; He lifted him to a leadership position and used his negative experiences not only for his own good but also for the benefit of his family.

The first thirty years of my life were filled with rejection and pain, but God has given me a life beyond my wildest dreams and has used my hurtful experiences for my benefit and for the benefit of others. Because I know pain of rejection and criticism, I have compassion and concern for those who suffer.

Day 57

Abide in My Love

*"Just as the Father has loved Me, I have
also loved you; abide in My love."*
John 15: 9

Many of us struggle to believe that God really loves us.
This could be for a variety of different reasons. For
some of us, it will be the result of past rejection and
the wrong belief that we are therefore unlovable. For
others, it may be that we cannot believe that God
would forgive us for some past weakness or failure. It
may be because we have a wrong image of God as
distant, critical and uncaring, like our own father. For
many of us, we can be so busy trying to earn
acceptance and love, that we fail to give the time for
this wonderful truth to penetrate and transform our
hearts and lives. We believe that love must be based
on performance and grade ourselves harshly,
comparing ourselves with others who appear to be
more attractive, popular and successful.

So how do we correct our failure to believe in God's
love? Here are several suggestions: if past rejection
makes us feel unlovable, we can choose to change our
perception of painful memories, recognising that the

person who rejected us was hurt and their behaviour had much more to do with their pain than any flaw in us. If we believe that we cannot be forgiven, consider the constant love and commitment that God demonstrated to the Israelites despite their continual rebellion and disbelief. Meditate on God's many promises to forgive us such as:

> *As far as the east is from the west, so far has He removed our transgressions from us.* (Psalm 103:12)

If our father was distant and uncaring, meditate on scriptures that describe God's character. Stop comparing ourselves unfavourably with others: we can all put on a good and successful face on the outside, but the truth may be very different.

Let us also consider how Jesus described His love for us: it is just the same as God's love for Him. There can be no greater love and this, and He demonstrated it by laying down His life for us. However, to know His love we need to abide in it, or immerse ourselves in it, just like a young child will throw himself into his father's arms and rest his head close to his father heart.

Day 58

I Can Do All Things

I can do all things through Him who strengthens me. Philippians 4:13

Most of us will have had experiences in our childhood when a parent or teacher spoke false and destructive statements about our lack of value and ability to succeed in life. We may have heard words such as: 'You are such a failure' or 'You will never succeed'. We may have had a brother or sister who appeared to be more successful or loved than we were. We may have been laughed at for being unattractive, or criticised for being too tall, or too short, or too fat, or too thin.

The tragedy is that these false and hurtful statements can affect our entire lives, forming an invisible barrier which blocks our progress and ability to live happy and fruitful lives. In most cases these words were probably untrue then and are certainly inappropriate now that we have grown into an adult, filled and empowered with God's indwelling presence.

Like the programming of a computer, these negative words – spoken to us when we were a child – have programmed our lives to believe something false about ourselves, and this programming needs to be changed. In order to change our false image of ourselves, we need to carefully and thoroughly evaluate what we really believe about ourselves. Even although the process may be painful, we need to face the negative and hurtful statements that were spoken to us and recognise that they had much more to do with the negative self-image of the person who spoke them and did not accurately describe us.

The next step is to renounce the lies and to choose to believe the truth. Take each false statement and declare out loud that this lie is not true and that you will not allow it to hold you back any longer. Find a scripture which corrects each lie and speak it to yourself daily, even if you do not initially believe it.

Each time that you do this the power of the lie will be reduced. We may have been told that we will never succeed, but the truth is that we are able to do all things because of the all-powerful in-dwelling presence of the Holy Spirit. God will never ask us to do anything which He will not also enable us to do.

Day 59

Greater is He

*You are from God, little children, and
have overcome them; because greater is
He who is in you than he who is in the
world.* 1 John 4:4

The above verse is part of a passage in which John is advising us to test the spirits in order to know whether they are from God. Let us, therefore, reflect on the reality of the spiritual world around us and how it seeks to infiltrate and control our lives. We may not have considered this seriously because our focus has been on what we can see with our physical eyes. However, the truth - whether we recognise it or not – is that the invisible spiritual world is continually seeking to influence our thoughts, words and actions.

In Romans 2, Paul urges us not to be confirmed to this world, but in our modern technically advanced generation, 'the world' is screaming at us from every direction, seeking to draw us into its vice-like grip. We are tempted to buy more and more possessions with the promise that they will improve the quality of our lives. We are persuaded that we have a right to receive a variety of different financial benefits and to claim compensation for even minor mishaps. We are encouraged to worship celebrities and to follow their often-destructive behaviour patterns. Even within the church, we find those seeking to lift themselves into the celebrity positions. We can seek to draw people into the kingdom by offering a multitude of benefits and forgetting that Jesus taught much about the cost of discipleship. This approach may bring people into the church but give them a false understanding of the gospel.

The good news is that the indwelling Holy Spirit is significantly greater that any ungodly influence which comes against us and so we do not need to fall victim to their influence and control. However, we will be continually tempted by the world, the flesh and the devil, and so we need to be alert and to listen to good teaching in order to avoid being deceived by them. However, John warns us that those who know God listen to sound teaching, but those who do not know God, do not want to listen to the truth and can therefore be deceived.

Day 60

Focus on What is Good

Finally, brethren, whatever is true,
whatever is honorable, whatever is right,
whatever is pure, whatever is lovely,
whatever is of good repute, if there is any
excellence and if anything worthy of
praise, dwell on these things.
Philippians 4:8

We will all face struggles, trauma and pain as a consequence of living in a fallen world. There is a spiritual battle waging between good and evil and any battle will produce casualties. However, 'in Christ' we can live a peaceful, secure, happy and fulfilled life if we follow biblical teaching. One example would be Jesus sleeping peacefully in a boat during a storm which terrified the disciples.

We all want to live peaceful, secure, happy and fulfilled lives, and spend much of lives striving to find this seemingly elusive and unobtainable desire. We think that it will be found by changing our circumstances – whether it is through acquiring money, or possessions, or celebrity status, or better relationships - but even if we do achieve these goals, we will find that they will never truly satisfy us. We can therefore spend our whole life seeking after these things only to find that they do not give what we desire.

The good news is that this peaceful, secure, happy and fulfilled life can be found by changing how we think, speak and act, and it is always possible for us to choose to think, speak and act differently. As God told the Israelites in Deuteronomy, chapter 30: His way to life and prosperity is not too difficult or out of our reach. God does not make false promises or give us impossible tasks.

In this above-quoted verse, Paul tells us to focus on what is true, honourable, right, pure, lovely and of good repute. The truth is that our thoughts will determine our emotional and mental health. If we focus on the pain, rejection and trauma that we have faced, we will be depressed and anxious. In direct contrast, if we focus our attention on all that has been good, and change our perspective of the negative events; looking for the benefits gained, the lessons learned and reminding ourselves that we survived each of these traumas, then our emotions will become more positive, peaceful, secure and happy.

Day 61

We Reap what we Sow

Now this I say, he who sows sparingly
will also reap sparingly, and he who sows
bountifully will also reap bountifully.
2 Corinthians 9:6

Do not be deceived, God is not mocked;
for whatever a man sows, this he will also
reap. For the one who sows to his own
flesh will from the flesh reap corruption,
but the one who sows to the Spirit will
from the Spirit reap eternal life.
Galatians 6:7-8

The above-quoted passages describe the biblical principle of sowing and reaping. The verb "to sow" indicates an investment. We sow seeds because we want to receive a harvest, or we invest into a business to gain financial benefits. We understand this principle when it is applied to agriculture and we can learn three lessons from doing so: first, if we want to receive a harvest, we need to plant some seed. Second, the size of our harvest depends on how many seeds we plant. Third, if we plant maize seeds, we will receive a harvest of maize but if we plant thistle seeds, we will receive a harvest of thistles.

We all understand and accept these three truths when we apply them to agriculture. However, we often find it hard to apply these same truths to our lives: we want to receive financial or material provision without first giving to God's work or to others and we believe that we can think, speak, and act in a negative way without it producing destructive consequences in our lives.

Paul describes this principle clearly: we will reap according to how we sow. When we sow little, we will reap little, but when we give generously, we will have all that we need and have enough for every good work. Also, when we act according to our sinful nature, we will reap destruction in our lives, but when we submit to the leading of the Holy Spirit, we will receive eternal life.

In conclusion, why is this good news: although life is unpredictable and we will face trials of many kinds, we are – in some measure – able to determine the course of our life by the choices that we make. If we consistently chose to give generously and to act righteously, we will ultimately reap good rewards.

Day 62

Guarded by Peace

Be anxious for nothing, but in everything
by prayer and supplication with
thanksgiving let your requests be made
known to God. And the peace of God, which
surpasses all comprehension, will guard
your hearts and your minds in Christ Jesus.
Philippians 4:6-7

In the past I have suffered from considerable anxiety and have experienced the very significant effects that anxiety can have on our physical bodies. I passed through one extremely difficult year which started with ill-health and a very serious reaction from some medication, and then spiralled downwards with anxiety, sleep deprivation and the increasing physical effects of anxiety.

Most anxiety is triggered from past trauma. This is often experienced in early childhood and no longer remains in our conscious memory. However, it does remain in our sub-conscious mind and when a similar event to the original trauma is experienced, our sub-conscious mind can react violently, causing anxiety, and even panic. We can then be confused by such a reaction because the trauma has been long forgotten, making the anxiety difficult to resolve.

Paul tells us not to be anxious and God never asks us to do the impossible. Let us, therefore, unpack this passage in order to understand how to obey it. The answer, I believe, lies in how we perceive life events. As a small child, any trauma will have a greater impact because of our immaturity and size, causing us to feel overwhelmed by the rejection, conflict or pain that we faced. Life without the knowledge of God's love and care, can make us feel like a victim.

Life lived close to God will be very different from our past experiences. God does not promise that our life with be trouble-free, but He does promise to be with us and to provide us with every resource that we need for every occasion. He does not, however, provide these resources until we need them and so we may not have the inner strength for an imagined trauma.

God's peace will guard us when we take our concerns to Him in prayer, update our perception of past events in light of His promised presence and care, stop worrying about what may happen, and thank Him that He will never fail us or forsake us.

Day 63

A Way Back

*"If I shut up the heavens so that there is no
rain, or if I command the locust to devour
the land, or if I send pestilence among My
people, and My people who are called by My
name humble themselves and pray and seek
My face and turn from their wicked ways,
then I will hear from heaven, will forgive
their sin and will heal their land."*
2 Chronicles 7:13-14

Throughout the Old Testament, we read of the
continual rebellion of the Israelites who disregarded
the numerous demonstrations of God's presence, love
and care and instead worshipped false idols
according to the custom and practices of the nations
who surrounded them. Time after time, God called
them back to Himself but after a short period of
renewal, they strayed again.

Sadly, we can look at the various idolatries practiced
during the Old Testament and fail to recognise the
multitude of ways in which we – even as Christian
believers – can also worship false gods. They may not
be gods fashioned of gold or stone, instead they are

gods of celebrity, consumerism, food, alcohol or drugs, to name just a few. Anything which we elevate to a position of worship and power over us, where we look to them to meet our emotional or physical needs becomes an idol, replacing God's rightful position in our lives.

In this above passage, we see a demonstration of God's amazing grace. Despite the constant rebellion of the Israelites, He is – once again – offering them a way back to His love and care. Humility and repentance are the doorways to healing and restoration: the humility to recognise and acknowledge how we have turned to idols instead of trusting God to act on our behalf, and repentance: the determination to eliminate these false idols from our lives.

This passage gives us hope even when facing devastating circumstances. We will all face tests and trials of various kinds. We will also face the consequences of our sin and for trusting in idols instead of worshipping God. However, regardless of the depth of our sin, His grace and mercy are always available for us. There is always a way back to His presence, love, protection, provision and care. No one has fallen too far for His grace and mercy to reach them.

Day 64

If My People!

"If I shut up the heavens so that there is no rain, or if I command the locust to devour the land, or if I send pestilence among My people, and My people who are called by My name humble themselves and pray and seek My face and turn from their wicked ways, then I will hear from heaven, will forgive their sin and will heal their land."
2 Chronicles 7:13-14

I would like to consider this same passage for a second day, and our focus will be on the relevancy of this promise. We live during a period in history when the world is suffering from severe weather conditions and the consequent suffering to whole communities. There is also much talk about climate change and how this will result in even more severe weather conditions in future. We may also remember that in three of the four gospels, Jesus promised that in the end times the world would suffer from a variety of major calamities, and these would include wars, famines, earthquakes and various plagues.

These extreme climatic disasters may therefore seem

inevitable and this Old Testament promise irrelevant. However, I have personally known of several climatic disasters where God has miraculously intervened to protect and to save areas when churches have turned to Him with praise and prayer. Furthermore, climate change can be seen as a result of man's greed and over-consumption of the world's resources, making this Old Testament promise very relevant today, and the need for repentance and prayer perhaps even more vital than it was in the time in which the Old Testament was written.

In conclusion, let me share three miraculous events that have taken place in communities which I know well. First, following an outbreak of Army Worm which devastated 70% of the crops in southern Malawi, this Army Worm did not invade the land where congregations had praised God in their fields each Sunday. Second, in an area where the rain had stopped and crops were dying, this area experienced five days on solid rain following prayer and praise in their fields. Third, very serious flooding, which had been forecast to move south, missed the area where congregations had turned to God in prayer.

Day 65

O Valiant Warrior!

The angel of the LORD appeared to him and said to him, "The LORD is with you, O valiant warrior..." The LORD looked at him and said, "Go in this your strength and deliver Israel from the hand of Midian. Have I not sent you?" He said to Him, "O Lord, how shall I deliver Israel? Behold, my family is the least in Manasseh, and I am the youngest in my father's house." Judges 6:12, 14-15

We have already considered how our perception of ourselves will determine our future. The New Testament describes how submitting to the lordship of Jesus will transform our lives. However, in direct contrast to embracing this truth about our position 'in Christ', we often continue to perceive ourselves according to our past: we see ourselves as we were without God, and especially when others abused us, criticised us, rejected us and ridiculed us.

In this Old Testament passage, we find Gideon describing himself in a negative way. He said that his family was the least in Manasseh and that he was the youngest in his father's house. His view of himself almost sabotaged the plans that God had for him, and our view of ourselves is likely to do the same. When God asks us to do something, we respond with numerous reasons why we cannot obey Him, and thus fail to enjoy the abundant life has He has planned for us. It was only because God continued to persuade Gideon that He would provide Him with all the strength and resources that he would need, describing him a valiant warrior, that Gideon was eventually persuaded to obey God's call, and as a result brought an end to the suffering of his people.

Perhaps God has plans for you to change your community or people in some other land, and through doing so, to lessen the pain and suffering in the world. God is love and does not enjoy watching people suffer. However, He chooses to work through us, whether it is through prayer or action and so He is looking for people through whom He can bring blessing, hope and joy instead of disaster, despair and pain. Will we therefore allow our negative perception of ourselves to continue to rob others of God's richest blessings are care?

Day 66

I searched for a Man!

"I searched for a man among them who would build up the wall and stand in the gap before Me for the land, so that I would not destroy it; but I found no one." Ezekiel 22:30

I believe that God would like us to continue with the thoughts included at the end of yesterday's study. As the unexpected thoughts expressed in the last paragraph came into my mind, I felt the strong emotion of love from the heart of God and the grief that He felt because of all the suffering that He witnessed on a constant basis. It took me by surprise. It is one of the most common questions that people ask: why does God allow so much suffering? I believe that part of the answer is found in these words spoken through Ezekiel.

God is a God of justice and He must, therefore, punish and discipline us when we sin. However, prayer and repentance can bring His abundant mercy and grace. Just as His justice required the death of Jesus to pay the price – death – for our sin, so God cries out for men and women who will stand in the gap between God and mankind. This phrase *'to stand in the gap'* appears to imply that it is possible for us to pray and to repent on behalf of others. God called Gideon to action in order to save his community; He spoke through Ezekiel to call for men and women to pray, and thus to follow Jesus' example: on the cross, He stood in the gap between God and man in order to save humankind.

I am not saying that all disasters are the result of God's discipline for sin. We live in a fallen world and we face a spiritual battle between good and evil. However, God is sovereign, and this passage shows that He desires to intervene if we will pray. God is love and does not want people to suffer. He is looking for people through whom He can bring blessing instead of disaster, whether it is through prayer, or action, or both.

Let us ask ourselves: do we doubt that God will answer our prayers? Does the suffering of others fail to move us? Do we lack confidence and faith in God's many promises to guide us, to strengthen us and to provide for us? Are our ears deaf to His call to change the community where we live and His promise that He will enable us to do it?

Day 67

For the Poor in Spirit

"Blessed are the poor in spirit, for theirs is the kingdom of heaven." Matthew 5:3

At first glance, this verse can – perhaps – appears a little negative. We can look at the word 'poor' and think of all the suffering caused by poverty or look back into church history when it raised poverty to a position to aspire to. It is true that Jesus did say that it would be as hard for a rich man to enter the kingdom of heaven as a camel to pass through the eye of a needle, but I do not believe that Jesus is referring to a financial position in this verse but to the confidence, or lack of confidence, in our ability to live independently from God.

We need to recognise that even as Christian believers, we can still live a life that is largely independent from God, struggling and striving to earn our salvation or to produce spiritual fruit through our own efforts and plans. We need, perhaps, to remind ourselves of Jesus' warning that we can only produce spiritual fruit if we abide in Him and that without Him, we can do nothing.

The phrase 'poor in spirit', as used in this verse, speaks of our recognition of this truth: that unless we abide in Jesus, we can do nothing. Now this is wonderfully good news. It removes all the fruitless stress, striving and exhausting self-effort, and replaces it with the incomparable joy and excitement of seeing God act in the most miraculous and world-transforming ways: events such as those we read about throughout the Old and New Testaments. Surely, this is what we all long for but often fail to see because of our proud and independent spirits – the very opposite to 'poor in spirit'.

Jesus also said that we should become like little children. Little children depend totally on their parents who they trust to care for them. Little children are 'poor in spirit'. Little children do not and cannot live independent lives. They are not able to make independent decisions or to determine what they will do each day. They yield to their parents' decisions and trust that they are the best for them. This is what God is asking from us and in return we will be overwhelmed by His love, grace and power flowing through our lives.

Day 68

Come to Me!

*"Come to Me, all who are weary and
heavy-laden, and I will give you rest."*
Matthew 11:28

We have already looked at this verse in an earlier study. However, there are more important considerations that we can gain from this promise spoken by Jesus. There is such a danger that we can simply read scripture in order to gain more head-knowledge. Scripture is, however, intended to transform us. We should not only read scripture but also apply it to our lives.

In this verse, we find an invitation and a conditional promise. We are asked to come, and if we do so, Jesus promises to give us rest. Let us first consider the deeper meaning of the word 'rest' because I believe that it means far more than just relaxation. It is also important to notice that if we do not fully understand what is being promised, we will never know whether we have received it, and thus become satisfied with less than God is offering us.

As human beings, it is generally accepted that we have three significant needs: to be secure (or loved), to be significant and to have a sense of self-worth. There is within each one of us a strong inner drive for these important needs. Without them we will be anxious and depressed. Without them, we will strive relentlessly to acquire or achieve them in ways which will never satisfy us. We look for them in money, possessions, food, alcohol, drugs, sex, success and celebrity status, to name just a few, but none of these will ever satisfy us. However much we have, we will always want more. This fruitless driven-ness is the opposite to a state of 'rest'. We only gain rest when these needs are met.

To come to a place of rest, we need to do two things: to come to Jesus and to believe that He will give us rest. True rest is only found in Him for only He can give us security, significance and self-worth. If we feel anxious, depressed or weary, we may have read this verse without applying this conditional promise to our lives. So, what does Jesus mean when He invites us to come? It means looking to Him to meet these three significant needs instead of striving to earn them or to receive them through our own independent efforts and plans.

Day 69

The Battle is not Ours

*...thus says the LORD to you, "Do not fear
or be dismayed because of this great
multitude, for the battle is not yours but
God's."* 2 Chronicles 20:15b

We have already considered this passage in the introduction of these studies. This whole chapter demonstrates the wonderful power of praise. Let us, once again, give an outline of this story: Judah was being attacked by foreign nations when Jehoshaphat was on the throne. In response, the king called the nation together and proclaimed a fast throughout Judah. After Jehoshaphat had prayed seeking God's help, Jahaziel gave a word of prophecy giving clear guidance to the people and promising to give them victory. He told them that they would not need to fight this battle, for the battle was not theirs but His!

For the whole of Judah, this was wonderfully good news! The Bible records that the multitude which had come against them was significantly larger than their own army, and so they knew that they desperately needed God's help if they were to avoid being massacred. This is the situation in which we find ourselves: we are opposed by forces of evil who are significantly greater and more powerful than we are, and without God's help, we will also be massacred.

If we return to this Old Testament story, we read that they appointed singers to go ahead of the army, and when they worshipped Him, God set ambushes and the enemy was defeated! This battle was won because the people of Judah responded to God's promise in faith and not fear. Their faith was demonstrated in two ways: first, they did not strive to fight this battle in their own strength because they placed their army behind the singers. Second, their praise demonstrated their faith that God was with them and would give them victory.

Similarly, we have nothing to fear because God will fight for us, just as He fought for Judah. He knows that we lack the strength to fight the multitude of evil forces who oppose us. Let us remind ourselves of John's teaching on this subject:

> You are from God, little children, and have overcome them; because greater is He who is in you than he who is in the world.
> 1 John 4:4.

Day 70

The Way Up is Down

"For everyone who exalts himself will be humbled, and he who humbles himself will be exalted." Luke 14:11

These words of Jesus warn us of the dire consequences of striving for a high position: if we try to exalt ourselves, God will humble us but if we humble ourselves, God will exalt us. Jesus confirms this in His parable of the Wedding Feast: if we take a place of honour we may be humbled and moved to a lower place, whereas if we take a lower place our host may move us to a higher place. If we want God to lift us to a position where we can achieve great things for Him, we need to take a lowly position. It is when we do so that God will lift us.

We find an excellent example of this in the life of Joseph. God allowed Him to be humbled through the action of his brothers and Potiphar, his master in Egypt. From his position as the favourite son, he was reduced to the position of a servant in a foreign land, and then even further to imprisonment in a foreign jail. However, God then exalted him to a leadership position, second only to Pharaoh and elevated him above his brothers who had abused him.

We also see this truth acted out in the life of Jesus. It is described clearly by John in his gospel and by Paul in his letter to the Philippians. Jesus did not hold on to His exalted position with God but humbled Himself and became like a servant. He not only washed the disciples' feet, telling us that we should do the same, but He humbled Himself even further through His death on a cross. We are told that it was because of His humble obedience, that God has exalted Him to the highest place and given Him a name above every name.

This teaching from Jesus is very good news because it removes the need for striving, self-promotion and self-effort: self-promotion will require us to make complex plans which will take considerable hard-work and sustained effort, while taking a humble position is easy and does not require any special talents or self-confidence. Furthermore, when we lift ourselves, we will have to maintain this elevated position, but when God exalts us, He will provide us with every ability and resource that we need and maintain the position for us.

Day 71

What is Love?

We know love by this, that He laid down
His life for us; and we ought to lay down
our lives for the brethren. 1 John 3:16

In this verse, John is teaching us how we can know genuine love. In Greek, the original language of the New Testament, there are four words for four different kinds of love: first, 'eros' is romantic or sensual love; second, 'storge' is the love within a family; third, 'philia' is the love between friends and fourth, 'agape' is the highest form of love, or God's love, which is pure, perfect, unconditional and sacrificial. John is teaching us that true love will sacrifice itself for others, and that we should therefore lay down our lives for others.

With the first three kinds of love there can be a selfish element to it, we love in order to receive something in return. We can also put conditions on whether someone is worthy to be loved: such as their appearance, character, behaviour, wealth or social status, to name just a few. Alternatively, we only love those who love us and treat us well and with respect. This is one reason why we can struggle to receive

God's love: we have only known conditional love.

In direct contrast, God's agape love is pure and without any selfish motivation. God loves us unconditionally. God's love is merciful, abundant, constant, everlasting, and unlimited. He does not love us in order to receive something back. We cannot earn it or deserve it. However, we do need to acknowledge our need of it and open our hearts to receive it by faith.

In the fourth chapter of his first letter, John tells us that 'God is love'. Everything that God does is motivated by a perfect and sacrificial love. He always acts in our best interest. He is patient with us when we make mistakes. He picks us up when we fall. He always sees the best in us and has good plans for our future, providing everything which we need to fulfil those plans. God chooses those who are weak, poor, disrespected and rejected by the world and lifts them into a place fruitfulness and significance. He is always with us and so we have no need to feel lonely or without help. Regardless of how we have been treated or described by others, God's love gives us value and significance.

Day 72

Lovingkindness

The LORD appeared to him from afar,
saying, "I have loved you with an
everlasting love; therefore I have drawn
you with lovingkindness." Jeremiah 31:3

Most of us, as Christian believers, would confess that we want to draw closer to God but do not know how to do so. We mistakenly think that God will require us to reach impossibly high standards of spirituality - spending hours and hours in prayer, or we dismiss ourselves as not being worthy of such a privilege and honour. These words of God spoken through Jeremiah should allay such mistaken fears. He tells us that He draws us closer to Himself with lovingkindness. There are three insights that we can gain from considering this phrase of just six words more closely, and we will do this over two days.

First, God is actively working to draw us closer to Himself. He desires to be near to us. Regardless of our low opinion of ourselves, He loves us and longs to put His arms around us just like a father lifting and holding his child close to his heart. There are two Bible verses in Old Testament which tell us that God had carried the Israelites. It is God who initiated the restoration of our relationship. While we were still sinners, He took the very painful and self-sacrificing step to eliminate the gulf between us. We did not look for Him, He looked for and found us. Just as He took the initiative to restore our relationship, so He also works to draw us closer to Him and He does this with lovingkindness. We only need to believe in and respond to His love.

Second, He draws us closer to Himself. He does not drive us from behind with a stick, as we would drive cows to find pasture or a sheep dog would round up sheep. Neither the cows nor the sheep are given a choice as to the direction which they take. In direct contrast, Jesus called His disciples with the words: 'follow Me'. In was an invitation, not a command. God goes ahead of us in order to prepare the way and He gives us complete freedom as to whether we will follow Him or not. God desires to bless us and to be close to us, but He always give us complete freedom to choose what kind a life we want to live.

Day 73

Drawing closer to God

*The LORD appeared to him from afar,
saying, "I have loved you with an
everlasting love; Therefore I have drawn
you with lovingkindness."* Jeremiah 31:3

Yesterday, we started to consider how God draws us with lovingkindness and we looked at two truths that we can learn from this phrase. First, God desires to draw us closer to Himself. We did not look for Him, but He searched for us. Second, He goes ahead of us to lead us and to draw us closer. He does not drive us from behind with a stick, giving us little choice as to whether we will obey Him, but gives us freedom to choose whether we will follow Him. Today, we will consider the third insight that we can learn from this short phrase.

Let us meditate on these words and consider what they are saying. We so often miss the richest truths in the Bible by reading the words quickly and not asking ourselves what they are really telling us. This phrase is teaching us that God's lovingkindness will draw us closer to Him. It is therefore true that the more we recognise and thank God for the multitude of blessings that He pours into our lives each day, the more we will love Him and quite naturally take steps to draw closer to Him. We can focus on His lovingkindness to two ways:

First, we should recognise and thank God for the many blessings that He pours on us each day. The fact that He has kept us alive until now, that the sun rises each morning and that we have air to breath, to name just three. Instead of focusing on the negatives, let us look for daily blessings to thank Him for. This will not only increase our faith and love for God but will also increase our joy.

Second, by confessing out biblical truth about God's lovingkindness. In direct contrast, we evaluate truth by our feelings and emotions which are volatile and unreliable. We feel unloved and so we confess, in words or thoughts, that we are not loved, increasing our faith that we are unlovable. Regardless of our feelings, we should confess biblical truth such as: 'I am abiding in God's love' or 'I am loved with an everlasting love' until our faith and feelings change. As we focus on God's lovingkindness, we will quite naturally draw closer to Him.

Day 74

Rooted and Grounded

...that He would grant you, according to
the riches of His glory, to be strengthened
with power through His Spirit in the
inner man, so that Christ may dwell in
your hearts through faith; and that you,
being rooted and grounded in love...
Ephesians 3:16-17

These two verses - together with following verses which we will consider tomorrow - form Paul's prayer for the church in Ephesus, and it emphasises the significance of our comprehending the extravagant love of God. It is when we understand and embrace God's love, that our lives are transformed. The whole prayer can be likened to climbing up a mountain in order to reach the summit. The summit is described as our being filled with all the fullness of God, and this should be the primary desire on every one of us. However, this blessing can only be reached by our taking each step as Paul describes them.

First, Paul uses the word 'grant', emphasising that these blessings cannot be earned or received through self-effort, they can only be given by God Himself. However, Paul also encourages our faith by reminding us of the 'riches of His glory'. God is generous and His resources are unlimited. We do not need to compete with one another as if there are inadequate resources to be fought over. There is more than enough for everyone to receive an abundant supply.

Second, Paul's first request was for the Ephesians to be strengthened through the Holy Spirit in their inner man so that Christ could dwell in their hearts. At the last supper Jesus spoke about the coming Holy Spirit: *"He will glorify Me, for He will take of Mine and will disclose it to you."* (John 16:14) It is the Holy Spirit who will reveal the truths about, and the presence of, Jesus to us.

Third, the indwelling Christ will enable us to be rooted and grounded in love. Just as a plant is anchored securely in the soil by its roots, and it is through the roots that the plant draws its nourishment from the soil enabling it to bear fruit, so it is as we put our roots down deeply into Christ, that His love gives us security and nourishment, enabling us to bear much fruit. As Jesus told His disciples in the gospel of John, we can only bear fruit when we abide in Him.

Day 75

Filled with God

*...may be able to comprehend with all the
saints what is the breadth and length
and height and depth, and to know the
love of Christ which surpasses
knowledge, that you may be filled up to
all the fullness of God.* Ephesians 3:18-19

These two verses follow those which we considered
yesterday and need to be considered with them. It is
only when we take the steps considered yesterday,
that we are enabled to receive the blessings promised
in these two above-quoted verses. It is only when
Christ dwells in our hearts and we are rooted and
grounded in His love that we will be able to more fully
comprehend the magnificence of His love and to be
filled with all the fullness of God.

Paul's fourth step is that are enabled to understand
the enormity of God's love. We have already
considered this very significant subject many times
because it is so vital to our maturity as a Christian
believer. However, we find it a hard truth to grasp
hold of because our only other experience of love is
the very limited and often selfishly motivated love of

family, friends and neighbours.

The summit of Paul's prayer is that we may be filled with God. All the previous steps are necessary because they change our focus from self to God, and this is essential because we cannot be filled with God while we are still filled with self. It is only as the Holy Spirit reveals the magnificence of Jesus to us and our thoughts and faith are built (rooted and grounded) more deeply in Him, that our selfish desires and interests will become less and less important.

The more we find our security (love), significance and self-worth in Jesus, the less we will need to acquire these three basis needs through selfish striving. As John the Baptist said: He must grow greater and I must become less. It is only as we know how deeply that we are loved by God and believe that He will take care of us, that we will be enabled to let go of self. This change will be a gradual process. The more we embrace God's love and faithfulness, the more we will recognise and thank Him for His love and daily care, leading us to trust less and less in ourselves and to be filled more and more with Him.

Day 76

The Fruit of the Spirit

But the fruit of the Spirit is love, joy, peace, patience, kindness, goodness, faithfulness, gentleness, self-control; Galatians 5:22-23a

True repentance requires us to recognise our fallen and selfish human nature and our strong tendency to live independently, striving unsuccessfully to make our lives work without God. Repentance is not only recognising and asking forgiveness for our independence and selfishness, but also committing ourselves to turn away from our sinfulness and to live a life that is pleasing to God. However, we will not be able to live righteously through self-effort alone.

If we are live a life that is pleasing to God, a life filled with joy and demonstrating the glory of God to a fallen world, we need to understand two significant and life-transforming truths. First, earlier in this above-quoted passage, Paul describes the deeds of the flesh as:

> *...immorality, impurity, sensuality, idolatry, sorcery, enmities, strife, jealousy, outbursts of anger, disputes, dissensions, factions,*

*envying, drunkenness, carousing, and things
like these...* Galatians 5:19b-21a

These behaviours are the fruit of a life that is lived independently from God, a life in which we are striving to find love, significant and self-worth through our own efforts. Let us remember that Jesus teaches us that we can judge a tree by its fruit. It is therefore true that these behaviours reveal an independent spirit and we will be unable to live a life which is pleasing to God until we look to Him to meet our needs.

Second, God never asks the impossible. It is true that turning to Christ will not eliminate our fallen human nature. This will remain within us, seeking to draw us back to our old way of living. However, the good news is that the indwelling Holy Spirit is significantly greater and more powerful than our old selfish and independent nature.

Instead, therefore, of focusing on our faults and weaknesses, let us confess out the truth even if we do not as yet demonstrate it: I am filled with love, joy, peace, patience, kindness, goodness, faithfulness, gentleness and self-control. Positive confession will build our faith in the truth of God's powerful indwelling presence and our behaviour will slowly change.

Day 77

The Glory of Jesus

God has chosen you from the beginning
for salvation through sanctification by
the Spirit and faith in the truth. It was
for this He called you through our gospel,
that you may gain the glory of our Lord
Jesus Christ. 2 Thessalonians 2:13b-14

In this passage from Paul's second letter to the church at Thessalonica, he describes one reason why God has chosen us: that we may gain the glory of Jesus. This is an extremely significant and almost unbelievable statement. We know that the New Testament encourages us to live a life which brings glory to God, just as Jesus glorified His father in everything that He did. We have also read about the resurrection and exaltation of Jesus, and that God has given Him a name above every name and that at His name, every knee will bow. However, this statement that we will gain the same glory as given to Jesus, seems completely impossible and totally inappropriate. How can we believe it?

Paul explains very clearly in this passage why and how this is true. He writes that it is through salvation and sanctification that we can receive this completely unwarranted honour and blessing. It is through salvation and sanctification that we are made worthy to receive the same glory as Jesus. Let us, therefore, meditate carefully on what these two words mean so that we can understand - and as a result - receive by faith the truth of this statement.

Salvation: through His death on the cross, Jesus took upon Himself our sinfulness, nailing the certificate of debt against us - which we were unable to pay - to the cross, and in return gave us His righteousness. Jesus' death paid the required price for all our sin, so that we are forgiven, and our sin has been completely removed as if we had never sinned. Salvation renders us holy.

Sanctification is the process through which God works within us to make the righteousness imputed to us through Jesus' death, a reality in our lives. Immediately we receive salvation, God perceives us as righteous regardless of our sinful behaviour. He then works in our lives to cleanse and sanctify us. It is through these two processes, that God makes us worth to receive Jesus' glory.

Day 78

Mine is Yours

*And he said to him, "Son, you have
always been with me, and all that is mine
is yours."* Luke 15:31

Before looking at this one verse, let us remind
ourselves of this whole parable. It is recorded in Luke
immediately following the parable of the Lost Sheep
and the Lost Coin. All three of these parables are told
to highlight God's immeasurable and unconditional
love for those who are lost, and – in the case of the
Prodigal Son – regardless of the depths of sin to which
they have fallen. It also emphasises that it is God who
searches for us. In fact: until He finds us, we do not
even know that we are lost or the depths to which we
have fallen.

In this parable, the younger of two sons asked his
father for his inheritance while his father was still
alive. He then left home, squandered his father's
money, and was left destitute and without friends. In
desperation, he got a job feeding pigs and would have
gladly eaten the pigs' food. Eventually he came to his
senses, returned home, asked for his father's
forgiveness and offered to become his servant. His

overjoyed father received him back as his son, dressed him in fine clothes and prepared a banquet in celebration of his return.

Meanwhile, the older son was working in the field and hearing the music, asked what was happening. A servant told him of his brother's return and of the banquet that had been prepared for him. In response, he became angry and refused to join the banquet despite his father's pleading him to do so. He complained to his father that despite his years of faithful service, he had never given him even a young goat to celebrate with his friends. I confess with shame that I have made a similar comment to God when I did not get my own way.

The main point of this parable is clear, but it includes many other lessons. It highlights the extravagant mercy, grace and generosity of God, as the father demonstrated to both brothers regardless of their behaviour. His whole estate was available to them both. In direct contrast, because we lack God's mercy and grace, we become jealous, competing and comparing ourselves with each other and judging others as being unworthy of God's richest blessings.

Day 79

Rich in Mercy

But God, being rich in mercy, because of
His great love with which He loved us...
Ephesians 2:4

In our modern consumer generation, the word 'rich' leads us to think first, and often exclusively, in terms of finances. We describe people as rich if they have great wealth, a mansion, beautiful clothing and a multitude of possessions. What as shame that our understanding of this word is so narrow. Surely, the truth is different. Instead of aspiring to gain these material blessings, which we will not be able to take with us when we die, our lives would be more blessed if we focused our attention on developing a character that is rich in mercy, love and peace for it is these attributes that will make us truly rich. God also requires us to show mercy to others if we are to receive His mercy.

Jesus told a parable about a rich man whose focus was on building larger barns in which to store his multitude of crops. He reminded the crowd who were listening to him of this man's foolishness and asked who would own all his possessions when he died. He ended this parable by saying that any person is foolish if he stores up material wealth and is not rich in his relationship with God. Jesus' advice is to focus our attention on those things which will have the greatest impact on our eternal destiny. So how do we develop an attitude of love and mercy? We look for opportunities every day to demonstrate love and mercy to those we meet, regardless of our feelings or their behaviour. We then offer these actions to God as a sacrificial gift, demonstrating our love for Him.

Paul tells us in this verse that it is because God loves us that He is rich in mercy towards us. God's great mercy – demonstrated so dramatically through Jesus' sacrifice and death - is evidence of His great love. It is possible to argue that it is God's wonderful love and mercy that has the greatest impact in our lives. He promises many other benefits when we draw closer to Him, but without His mercy, we would not be able to receive them. It is His mercy which opens the door to every blessing available to us in Christ. It is His mercy which restores our broken relationship with Him and lifts us to a place equal to His Son.

Day 80

Do We have a Vision?

*Where there is no vision, the people are
unrestrained...* Proverbs 29:18a

The above-quoted verse from the book of Proverbs warns us of the danger of having no vision. The consequence of living without a vision is recorded in several translations as the people running unrestrained. In the New King James and the Amplified versions, this phrase is translated with the far more serious consequence of death. In the Geneva version, the word used is 'decay'.

When we do not have a goal or vision for our life, we will lack purpose and consequently have little reason to get up each morning. We will wonder around aimlessly, allowing ourselves to be drawn this way and that way by circumstances, or the influence of family and friends. Furthermore, when life is difficult – and none of us will escape problems of one kind or another – we can be tempted to despair and depression. In direct contrast, when we have a God-given goal which we feel passionate about, we will not allow ourselves to be led away in a different direction or to give up when we face tests and trials.

I have recently moved into a new house where the garden had been neglected and was filled with heavy clay and builders' rubble. As a result, it filled with water when it rained heavily, and many plants would have died. However, I was determined to construct a beautiful garden. This meant digging out the clay and rubble and adding manure and topsoil. It was extremely hard work and it rained very heavily that winter making the clay sticky and difficult to work. Most days I got wet and was covered with mud, but I persevered because I had a vision of a beautiful garden which I was determined to achieve.

The good news is that God has a vision or ministry for each of us which has been especially prepared for us personally and is appropriate to our character, interests and gifting. Furthermore, God will provide every resource and gifting needed for us to fulfil His plan for our life. I have found that when I try to build my own ministry or to meet my own needs through my own plans and efforts, it fails miserably but when I allow God to lead me, the results are glorious.

Day 81

Walk in Love

*...and walk in love, just as Christ also
loved you and gave Himself up for us, an
offering and a sacrifice to God as a
fragrant aroma.* Ephesians 5:2

In this verse, Paul exhorts us to love others in the same way as Jesus loves us. Throughout His life, Jesus set an example for us to follow. This statement may appear an obvious one and yet we often fail to apply this wonderful truth to our lives. We gain two significant benefits from doing so.

First, everything which He did during His three years of public ministry demonstrated His love for us. It is well said that action is more powerful than words. It is therefore true that if we struggle to believe in His love for us, then we should meditate on His life, and especially on His death. In everything He did, He demonstrated love and compassion to those who surrounded Him. He was always sensitive to the needs of others, whether it was for healing or for food. His teaching showed us how to live abundantly. He humbled Himself to the position of a servant, paid little attention to His own comfort or reputation and was prepared to suffer agony on the cross for our blessing and benefit.

Second, Paul tells us to follow Jesus' example of demonstrating self-sacrificing love to others. At first glance, this may well appear challenging, but the truth is that it will be the source of much blessing. To understand this, we need to know one important New Testament principle: God will treat us in the same way as we treat others.

Let us look a three examples: God will forgive us as we forgive others (Matthew 6:15), God will judge us as we judge others (Matthew 7:2), and God will provide for us in the same measure as we give to others (Luke 6:38). I have also found that when we focus on lifting and encouraging others, God will lift, promote and encourage us. However, the opposite is also true: when we try to lift ourselves, God will humble us (Luke 14:11).

Finally, Paul teaches us that Jesus' sacrifice was a fragrant aroma to God. We can therefore, I believe, trust that all our self-sacrificing and loving actions to others will also be a fragrant aroma to God which will bring glory to Him.

Day 82

No Spot or Wrinkle!

*...that He might present to Himself the
church in all her glory, having no spot or
wrinkle or any such thing; but that she
would be holy and blameless.*
Ephesians 5:27

Paul includes this verse within a longer passage about marriage and following his exhortation to husbands to love their wives in the same way as Jesus loves the church. Once again, we are given a clear example of the very high standards that God requires from us. Even while we were still sinners, Jesus laid down his life so that we - through His death - could be made holy. God is therefore asking husbands to offer this same self-sacrificing love to their wives.

Several verses in the New Testament can be interpreted to imply that we, as the church, are being prepared to be the bride of Christ. Perhaps the clearest is in the book of Revelations:

*Let us rejoice and be glad and give the glory
to Him, for the marriage of the Lamb has
come and His bride has made herself ready.*

> *It was given to her to clothe herself in fine
> linen, bright and clean; for the fine linen is
> the righteous acts of the saints.* Revelation
> 19: 7-8

This verse from Ephesians could be understood as a description of Jesus presenting us to Himself as His bride, dressed in a beautiful and spotlessly white wedding dress; holy, blameless and without any impurity or defect.

What an amazing honour, that God has chosen us to be a bride for His Son. I am reminded of the well-known children's story of Cinderella. She was cruelty treated by her stepmother and two stepsisters who forced her to do all the servants' work. One day she met a handsome stranger who was really the king's son in disguise, and after being miraculously enabled to attend a ball held by the king to find a bride for his son, the prince - who had fallen in love with her - searched for her and married her. Cinderella is therefore elevated from the position of an abused servant to a princess, from a kitchen to a palace, and from rags to riches.

Surely, this is exactly what God has done for us and Paul confirms the amazing transformation that God has made possible for us through the death of His son and His work of sanctification in our lives.

Day 83

Buried with Him

...having been buried with Him in
baptism, in which you were also raised
up with Him through faith in the working
of God, who raised Him from the dead.
Colossians 2:12

In this verse, Paul is using the symbolism of baptism to help us to understand, and therefore to believe and to receive by faith, the transformation that God has so graciously achieved for us through Jesus' crucifixion, burial and resurrection. Let us therefore look at the picture that Paul is presenting to us.

First, let us consider the events preceding and following Jesus' death. In the Garden of Gethsemane, Jesus – who is perfect in every way - took upon Himself the sin of every one of us. Although He is perfect, He became sin for us and took the full punishment for our sin: death. Although He was entirely innocent, He died in agony on the cross in order to restore our relationship with God. Following His death, He was buried but on the third day He rose again and appeared to all the disciples before ascending into Heaven forty days later.

Second, as Jesus died in our place, it is as if we died

with Him. As Paul wrote in his letter to the church at Galatia:

> *I have been crucified with Christ; and it is no longer I who live, but Christ lives in me; and the life which I now live in the flesh I live by faith in the Son of God, who loved me and gave Himself up for me.* Galatians 2:20

This is the symbolism of baptism. As we go down into the water, it represents our death and burial. As we come up out of the water, it represents our being raised from death and being lifted to a new life.

Third, we need to apply this truth into our lives by faith. If we want to be raised to a new life, we first need die to self and to live by faith for God. We need to put into action the symbolism of our baptism. The more we identify with Jesus' death and burial, the more we will be raised with Him into a new and spiritually abundant life.

We identify with Jesus' death by letting go of our selfish and independent lifestyle in which we trusted in our own very limited abilities and resources, and submit to the lordship of Jesus, following His example, going wherever He leads us, and trusting in His ability and resources.

Day 84

God is in your Midst

The LORD your God is in your midst, A
victorious warrior. He will exult over you
with joy, He will be quiet in His love, He
will rejoice over you with shouts of joy.
Zephaniah 3:17

There are three wonderful blessings included in just this one verse, each of which will make a significant difference to our lives and so we will consider it over two days. First, God is in our midst as a victorious warrior. Sooner or later we will find ourselves facing very difficult situations which make us feel weak, vulnerable, lonely, anxious, depressed and overwhelmed.

We feel these negative emotions because, even as Christian believers, we can live largely independent lives, trusting in our own resources, and looking at our circumstances according to our own perception of our current situation. God may therefore allow us to face difficult circumstances where we are forced to face up to our limitations and false perceptions so that we recognise our need to draw upon His constant presence and promised guidance and help.

At the time of writing this meditation, the world is facing the coronavirus pandemic and governments are being forced to take unprecedented steps to reduce the growth of this disease which is currently killing thousands of people and threatening to overwhelm even the very best national medical facilities. Populations throughout the world are therefore being forced to isolate themselves with all the consequent results of loneliness, loss of income and business failure, as well as facing the very real risk of an early death.

This situation threatens to overwhelm even the most resilient person. It is at times like this when we need to meditate on this amazing truth: God is in our midst as a mighty warrior. Our circumstances may overwhelm us, but they will not overwhelm Him. He is victorious and sovereign in every situation and He will enable us to be victorious however difficult our circumstances. God does not promise to protect us physically, but He does promise that we can remain at peace and overcome negative emotions in every situation. We overcome by recognising His constant victorious and sovereign presence.

Day 85

Quiet in His Love

The LORD your God is in your midst, A
victorious warrior. He will exult over you
with joy, He will be quiet in His love, He
will rejoice over you with shouts of joy.
Zephaniah 3:17

We looked yesterday at the wonderful truth that God is in our midst, a victorious warrior. The three following phrases in this verse should be looked at together. With the second part of this verse, different English versions of the Bible translate them quite differently although they can all be summed up with this paraphrase: God will exult over us with joy because He will be silent, making no mention of our past sins, or even recalling them. Zephaniah is confirming God's words spoken through both Isaiah and Jeremiah to say that He will forgive or blot out our sins and not remember them anymore.

It would be beneficial, perhaps, to compare this promise with our own behaviour towards those who have sinned against us. We know that we need to forgive them, but it is difficult not to remember what they did to us. We often choose to forgive but not to forget. Whenever we are faced with that person, the memory of what they did comes flooding back and can scar our thoughts and evaluation of them for a long time. It is easy, therefore, to think that God behaves in the same way: that although He forgives our sins, His evaluation of us will continue to be negatively affected by our past failures.

Isaiah, Jeremiah, and Zephaniah are all telling us that God rejoices over us because He chooses not to remember our sins or to allow our past behaviour to negatively affect our future. We, for example, might not choose a certain person for a job because we know that they failed the last time that we asked them to do something. We remember their past poor performance. God does not act in this way.

When He looks at us, it is as if we had never sinned. His attitude towards us in always positive. He continually gives us a second opportunity. He never gives up on us because we have failed Him before. He does not choose a ministry for us based on our past failure, behaviour, ability or performance, but on our potential in Him. When He calls us, He equips us.

Day 86

Riches of Grace

In him we have redemption through his blood, the forgiveness of sins, in accordance with the riches of God's grace that he lavished on us. With all wisdom and understanding... Ephesians 1:7-8

As we read these verses, it is as if Paul is struggling to find adequate words to describe God's amazing goodness and mercy. He speaks about the riches of His grace which He lavishes upon us. We know that God is a God of Justice and justice requires that sin must be punished. Let us for a moment, imagine a world where there is no police force or justice system and so criminals can cause immense suffering and loss to the rest of the population without any possibility of their criminality being stopped. What a dark and fearful world this would be for all those of us who would like live honest and peaceful lives.

Justice is very important, but God is also a God who loves us unconditionally and wants to lavish His richest blessings upon us. It is because of the enormity of His love for us that He gave up His one and only Son to extremely suffering and death and to take the punishment for our sin so that He can lavish His grace upon us. God's grace means that we do not receive the punishment that we deserve but we do receive the blessing which we do not deserve. In this way God can demonstrate both His justice and His abundant love regardless of depths of sin to which we may have fallen. However extreme our sinfulness, Jesus has taken the full punishment for it. There is no one who is beyond the reach of God's love and offer of complete restoration and transformation.

Jesus described God's grace in His parable of the Prodigal Son. This son had acted in a very disrespectful and selfish way towards his father and had wasted the inheritance that his father had so generously given him. And yet, when he came to his senses and returned home, humbled and repentant, his father treated him as if he had never sinned and he was restored completely back into the heart of his family. The amazing grace shown by the father was too much for his other son who appeared to lack the compassion and mercy of his father. This grace which God shows to us, He asks us to show to others.

Day 87

He first loved Us

We love, because He first loved us.
1 John 4:19

I have learned over many years that love is the elixir
of life. I have tried in so many ways to find peace and
happiness with extremely limited success. My own
efforts may have given some brief joy but it never
lasts because however much I achieve or acquire, it is
never enough and I find that I am very quickly looking
for the next thing to buy or to achieve. The one thing
that has given me most sustained joy is expressing
and demonstrating love to God and to others. As Paul
wrote in his first letter to the Corinthians: love never
fails.

Paul tells us in this passage that we are enabled to
love because God first loved us. As we allow God to
pour His love into our hearts and lives, it will
transform us and overflow into the lives of those
around us. Knowing that we are loved will enable us
to take our eyes off ourselves and our perceived
needs and focus instead on God and other people. The
more we recognise how much God loves us, the more
we will want to pour out our thanks to Him, and the

more that we thank Him for His love, the greater our sense of being loved will become.

Sadly, our lives may have been devoid of love, with those who should have loved us either rejecting us, criticising us or abusing us. Any child who grows up without love, will find it difficult to believe and to receive God's love. So how can we turn this situation around? Thankfulness is the key. Look every day for small demonstrations of His love. Look at nature and its beauty and remind yourself that God created it for our provision and joy.

Remind yourself that He has kept you alive until this time and has enabled you survive many difficult or even dangerous situations. Thank Him for sacrificing His own Son for our sake and for our salvation and compete restoration. Search for and thank Him for the many promised blessings that He gives us in His Word.

The more blessings we find to thank God for, the greater our sense of being loved and valued will become, and the easier we will find it to love others, even those who have hurt us or abused us. Similarly, the more we express and demonstrate love to others, the greater and more sustained will be our joy.

Day 88

I have been Crucified

I have been crucified with Christ; and it is no longer I who live, but Christ lives in me; and the life which I now live in the flesh I live by faith in the Son of God, who loved me and gave Himself up for me.
Galatians 2:20

In this verse, Paul is confessing out his faith in the truth of what has already taken place for all those of us who have made Jesus our Lord and Saviour. Because He died in our place, it is as if we have been crucified. He suffered all the pain inflicted on a body during crucifixion in our place, but we gain all the benefits of His suffering. By responding in faith to the gospel message, we accept that our self-life has been put to death. This is the symbolism of baptism: that we have been put to death and have been buried in order that – like Jesus – we may rise to a new life. Death to self must precede a risen life.

Our self-life has been put to death in order that Jesus' indwelling presence may been demonstrated through our lives. Although Jesus already lives within us, if 'self' remains alive, it will block a demonstration of

His presence. We cannot defeat our self-centredness by self-effort but by faith in what God has already done for us. Paul said:

> *Therefore if anyone is in Christ, he is a new creature; the old things passed away; behold, new things have come.*
> 2 Corinthians 5:17

We will live a transformed and victorious life when we understand and receive by faith what God has already achieved for us.

We often live defeated lives because we are reluctant to put our self-life to death. We long for a demonstration of God's presence, but we also want to keep 'self' alive. Paul was happy to die to self because he knew that God loved him and gave Himself up for him. When we know that someone loves us and wants the best for us, we are enabled to trust them and to put our lives into their hands.

We see this in families where children know that they are loved. These children do not worry about whether their parents will care for them and protect them. I doubt whether they even think about it. When we know God loves us, we will no longer feel the need to protect and promote 'self'.

Day 89

No longer Slaves to Sin

...knowing this, that our old self was
crucified with Him, in order that our
body of sin might be done away with, so
that we would no longer be slaves to sin,
for he who has died is freed from sin.
Romans 6:6-7

In these two verses Paul is confirming the truth which
we considered yesterday: that we were crucified with
Christ. In these verses, Paul gives us further benefits
of this wonderful but challenging truth. We
considered yesterday how, as we put our self-life to
death by faith, we are raised to a new life but
emphasised that death must precede a resurrection
life.

Paul teaches us that because we were crucified with
Christ, our body of sin no longer has any power over
us. This is wonderful news. We do not defeat sin by
self-effort but by faith in the truth: that in Christ, our
body of sin has been put to death. However, we must
choose to walk in this truth.

Our self-centredness no longer has any power over us

unless we choose to give it power. God has given us victory, but we need to choose to walk in it.

We considered yesterday how baptism symbolises our choice to put our self-life to death by faith in order that we may rise to a new resurrected and sin-free life. However, as new believers, we often fail to understand the choice that we are making when we get baptised. This truth should perhaps be taught more clearly to all those who want to get baptised. Baptism should be confirmation of our decision to die to self, to follow Christ and to live for Him instead of living for ourselves. As Jesus prayed in the Garden of Gethsemane:

> *...saying, "Father, if You are willing, remove this cup from Me; yet not My will, but Yours be done."* Luke 22:42

We do not defeat sin by self-effort but by confessing out the truth that sin has been put to death and no longer has any power over me. We choose to put off the old self and to put on the new resurrected life. Once Jesus has chosen to God's will instead of His own, we read:

> *Now an angel from heaven appeared to Him, strengthening Him.* Luke 22:23

God will also strengthen us when we make this same choice.

Day 90

The Lord stood with Me

At my first defense no one supported me,
but all deserted me; may it not be
counted against them. But the Lord stood
with me and strengthened me...
2 Timothy 4:16-17a

Even though we join a world-wide family when we become a Christian, a life which is totally sold-out for God can be a very lonely one. It is sadly true that not every believer wants to step out and to take very real risks in their pursuit of God, and many would prefer a comfortable and safer life in which they are still largely in control. I would compare it with Peter stepping out of the boat and onto the water while the rest of the disciples remained in the boat.

The tragedy of this event is that Peter was far safer than his colleagues because if a severe storm had battered the boat, it may have sunk, whereas Jesus' word and His outstretched hand would have held Peter up. It would appear from Paul's words that his determination to follow Jesus whatever the risk and the cost, had resulted in many of his colleagues deserting him.

However, Paul's experience was that Jesus had stood with him and strengthened him, and we can be confident that this will be our experience as well. God will never lead us into any situation and then leave us to struggle alone. Jesus called his disciples to follow Him and so He will always go ahead of us to prepare the way for us and to show us where to go and what to do. He does not expect us to work the route out for ourselves and, because He walks ahead of us, He will also warn us when there is danger ahead.

At the time of writing this study, the world is facing the Covid 19 pandemic with all the difficulties and dangers faced by so many people. Towards the end of last year, before the first case in China, God spoke to me and said that we would be passing through a very difficult time and He was asking me to write these studies so that they could help us to stay positive and full of faith during this very difficult time. I thought that He meant sometime in the future, not the following year. God knows exactly what the future holds and if we stay close to Him, He will prepare us for what lies ahead and walk through it with us.

Day 91

Learning to be Content

*I am not saying this because I am in need,
for I have learned to be content whatever
the circumstances. I know what it is to be
in need, and I know what it is to have
plenty. I have learned the secret of being
content in any and every situation,
whether well fed or hungry, whether living
in plenty or in want.* Philippians 4:11-12
(NIV)

During this Covid 19 pandemic, life has become restricted and difficult with thousands of deaths and great financial hardship. Paul's words are therefore very significant. I do not want to undermine the suffering faced by so many, but we can learn important lessons from Paul, who had faced great suffering.

Paul wrote that he had learned to be content. Contentment is something which needs to be learned, it does not come naturally. Our natural inclination is always to want more – whether that is achievements, finances, or possessions. However, as Paul also wrote: *But godliness with contentment is great gain.* (1 Timothy 6:6 NIV) I have found great benefits from being content and I have learned it during this pandemic. I have learned to enjoy the few things which I CAN do, like the beauty of nature, growing plants, and vegetable seeds, and even washing-up! As a result, I have felt overwhelming peace, joy, and gratitude, something which I had lacked when I enjoyed greater freedom.

Let us consider four reasons why contentment will bring great gain. First, happiness is not found in having or achieving more. If we want more, we will focus on what we do NOT have, and this will make us frustrated and miserable. In contrast, if we are grateful for what we DO have, this will make us happy.

Second, the more we recognise and thank God for the blessings we enjoy, the more our faith in Him will grow, and increased faith will bring even greater blessings.

Third, when we have abundant possessions it is easy to depend on them, but their benefits are limited. However, when we have little, we are more likely to depend on God, whose blessings and resources are unlimited.

Fourth, when we depend on our own resources, they can be lost, stolen, or destroyed, but when we depend on God, His presence and help can never be taken away.

Day 92

When Less is More

I am not saying this because I am in need,
for I have learned to be content whatever
the circumstances. I know what it is to be
in need, and I know what it is to have
plenty. I have learned the secret of being
content in any and every situation,
whether well fed or hungry, whether living
in plenty or in want.
(Philippians 4:11-12 NIV)

It is important for us to understand the up-side-down nature of the gospel. However, the truth is that it is the world, and not the gospel, which is the wrong way up. Failing to understand how different the gospel is to the world and the culture in which we live, can rob us of the many blessings promised to us in scripture. We have looked at some of these in earlier studies. Today we will look at why we can thank and praise God even when we have little.

In a generation and culture in which we are bombarded with almost constant advertising, we may be deceived into believing that acquiring more, whether it is finances, possessions, clothing, larger houses, or luxury holidays – to name just a few, is something to strive for. The very opposite is true. As we considered yesterday, happiness is not found in having more but in appreciating and enjoying what we have. Paul had experienced both being in need and having plenty and was content with either.

The truth is that in our hectic lives in which we rush around trying to acquire or achieve more, we miss out on so much because we are too busy to notice them. Also, when we have more, we can trust in these instead of in God. It is often true that a simpler, less cluttered, and more peaceful life with less is better. Let us remember how Gideon defeated the Midianites with a reduced army of just three hundred men.

When we live at a slower pace, we will have time to draw closer to God; to enjoy the beauty of nature; to become more sensitive to the needs of other people; and these will improve our enjoyment of life. After a time when I have been denied some of the blessings which I have taken for granted, I enjoy them so much more. For example, a shower and an ice-cold drink after spending a week or so in the sweltering heat and lack of these facilities in rural Africa.

Day 93

New every Morning

*The LORD's lovingkindnesses indeed never
cease, For His compassions never fail.
They are new every morning; Great is
Your faithfulness.* Lamentations 3:22-23

We considered these two verses in an earlier study
but there are further encouraging lessons that we can
draw from them. Today we will focus on the unlimited
nature of God's loving kindness and compassion.
Jeremiah uses three phrases to emphasise this: first,
they never cease; second, they never fail; and third,
they are new every morning. God's supply of loving
kindness and compassion will never run out.

Regardless of how many times we fail or the depth of
our sin, God will continue to love us and to show
mercy to us. In contrast to the stock of certain items
in a shop which will run out if too many people buy
them on the same day, God's supply of love is never
exhausted.

Our experience with our parents, friends or work
colleagues may have been different. As fallible human
beings, our love and mercy can be limited, and we are

likely to have faced circumstances where someone has treated us harshly because of some small failure or weakness, and this failure to live up to some else's high expectations has then resulted in long-term relationship difficulties with that person. Consequently, we can expect God to behave in a similar way.

Very often a problem lies in our inability to forgive ourselves. This mistake or failure may have taken place many years ago, and yet we still judge and criticise ourselves for what we did or did not do. Because we cannot forgive ourselves, we do not believe that God can forgive us either and we falsely conclude that He will never use us in any significant way. We write ourselves off as a permanent failure without any hope that things can change.

We need, therefore, to take Paul's words very seriously. God is a God of the second, third, fourth, fifth, sixth, seventh, eight, nineth and tenth chance. We can never exhaust the depths of His mercy. It is new every morning as if we have never sinned. He never writes us off as a hopeless failure. He is always ready to offer us a new beginning with exciting ministry opportunities.

Day 94

Channels of God's Love

*Love never fails;... But now faith, hope,
love, abide these three; but the greatest of
these is love.* 1 Corinthians 13:8a,13

It has taken me forty years to understand the importance of love above all other gifts. As Paul wrote: love never fails and is greater than faith and hope. He also wrote earlier in this passage that any gifting, if it does not operate in love, is worthless. I have read a few near-death testimonies when the writers were confronted with just one question: how much have you loved others?

God, I believe, longs to demonstrate His love and mercy to a hurting world and is looking for channels through whom He can pour His blessing and grace. The only requirement for an effective channel is that it must be prepared to be hollowed out in order to become a conduit for His love and power. The more each channel is hollowed out, the greater the flow of His power through it.

Many years ago, I heard a sermon illustration of this truth. There was a farmer whose crops were wilting through lack of rain. Knowing that there was a river nearby, he carefully considered how he could transfer this water to his crops. He noticed that there was a bamboo plant growing beside his fields. It was a magnificent plant, growing tall and strong with an abundance of green leaves.

This plant, he thought, could be the answer. He therefore approached the plant and cut down ten stems with his knife. He trimmed off all the magnificent leaves and split the stems carefully in half down their length. He then hollowed out the centre of the stems and laid these split and hollowed stems on the ground so that the water from the river could flow along them to his crops.

This describes the process by which God prepares us to be channels of His love. He does not choose us because of our appearance, education, wealth, or gifting. Instead, He looks for those who will allow Him the freedom to make them into vessels which he can use for His glory. The good news about being used as a channel for God's love, is that a channel gets very wet! The more we empty ourselves of self and love others, the more God will fill us with His love.

Day 95

A Pathway to Joy

*"A new commandment I give to you, that
you love one another, even as I have
loved you, that you also love one another.
By this all men will know that you are My
disciples, if you have love for one
another."* John 13:34-35

We will spend a second day considering the importance of love above all things. We all know how wonderful it is to be loved. It helps us to recognise our true value and significance. When we feel good about ourselves, it will also motivate us to live a more abundant and satisfying life. Knowing that we are loved is an essential need for our physical and mental well-being. However, there is even greater blessing to be gained from demonstrating love to others.

There are some days when I wake up feeling mildly depressed and lacking in joy. The world does not appear quite so wonderful as it did yesterday! If I then pray and ask God to show me how I can demonstrate love to someone that day, I have found that He will quickly bring thoughts and ideas into my mind, and as I consider them and how I can put them into action, my mood is immediately and dramatically transformed. As I consider ways that I can demonstrate love to those around me, it is as if a spring of exuberant joy bubbles up from my heart. Let us also remind ourselves of the many scriptures which promise that God will treat us in the same say as we treat others.

Jesus promises that people will recognise that we are His disciples when we love each other. Certainly, I have found that it can be an open doorway to share the gospel with others.

When I am out in public, I look for opportunities to compliment people around me. I may compliment someone on their clothing, their hairstyle, their children, their baby, their dog, or something which they are saying or doing. It is such an easy way to start a conversation with a stranger. It very often lifts their mood and can lead to them becoming open to discuss more sensitive and spiritual matters. I do not think that there is anyone who will not respond positively and openly to a compliment.

Day 96

Grasshoppers!

We saw the Nephilim there (the descendants of Anak come from the Nephilim). We seemed like grasshoppers in our own eyes, and we looked the same to them. Numbers 13:33

Many of us will be able to relate to the experiences of the Israelites as they walked round and round in circles in the wilderness. We may not face the same trials as the Israelites, but most of us will face testing times such as ill health, physical handicap, financial hardship, hunger and crop failure, marriage and relationship breakdown, physical, emotional or sexual abuse, bullying or rejection, and fail to see the break-through promised in Scripture.

A desert is not a comfortable place to live in and God never intended that the Israelites should stay there. Their journey should only have taken eleven days, but they remained there for forty years until all that generation except for Joshua and Caleb had died. It has been said that God had led them out of Egypt, but

He needed to get Egypt out of the Israelites. Even though He had set them free from their cruel oppressors, they still thought and behaved like slaves.

The Israelites were used to being controlled by cruel and oppressive masters and found it difficult to believe in their freedom and to trust in the goodness and faithfulness of God. They continued to see themselves as weak and vulnerable slaves and so when Moses sent the twelve spies to explore the land, ten of them saw themselves as grasshoppers as compared with the inhabitants of the Promised Land.

In a similar way, one reason why we can walk round and round in circles in our own wilderness experiences is because we continue to see ourselves as we were before God rescued us and transformed us through Jesus' death on the cross. Although God has liberated and empowered us, we can continue to struggle with feelings of inferiority, anxiety, frustration, despair, and disbelief.

The good news is that we are completely new creatures in Christ. The person that we were has gone. We are no longer slaves to sin nor weak and vulnerable. In Christ, we are filled and empowered by the Holy Spirit to walk victoriously through any situation.

Day 97

God is Good

Now the serpent was more crafty than any beast of the field which the LORD God had made. And he said to the woman, "Indeed, has God said, 'You shall not eat from any tree of the garden'..." The serpent said to the woman, "You surely will not die! For God knows that in the day you eat from it your eyes will be opened, and you will be like God, knowing good and evil." Genesis 3:1,4-5

God is good, He loves us and wants the best for us. However, although we often confess this as a truth, it is not always a truth that we believe deep down in our hearts. This is because it is one of Satan's strategies to deceive us in this area. If he can cause us to believe the lie that God is not good and does want the best for us, we become vulnerable to his temptations to trust in ourselves and our own strategies to improve our lives, just as he did with Adam and Eve.

If we look at Satan's conversation with Eve, we find him insinuating that God is not good: first, he asks whether God had forbidden them from eating from any tree in the garden when God had only forbidden them from eating from one tree. This question is suggesting that God had surrounded them with good things but was depriving them of the enjoyment of eating any of them.

Second, he told her that she would not die if she ate from the forbidden tree, suggesting that God is a liar and that His Word cannot be trusted. Third, he told her that the forbidden fruit would make her like God, implying that God had prohibited them from eating something which not only looked good, but which would also bring significant improvement to their lives.

In this passage we find Satan maligning God's character in three areas: first, He does not want us to enjoy ourselves. Second, He lies, and we cannot believe what He says. Third, He denies us things which will benefit us. He will try to deceive us in a similar way, tempting us to trust in ourselves and our own limited resources.

It is important that we recognise his strategy and resist his false insinuations. Let us decide today to believe the truth and not the lie. Even when circumstances appear to deny it, let us choose to believe that God is good.

Day 98
Who can be against Us?

*What, then, shall we say in response to
these things? If God is for us, who can be
against us?* Romans 8:31 (NIV)

We have considered how Jesus did not promise us an
easy or trouble-free life. Quite the opposite, for He
warned us that we would face trouble in this world.
Jesus faced opposition, condemnation and
crucifixion, the first-century church faced severe
persecution, and all through history Christians have
faced persecution, torture, and martyrdom.
Surprisingly, it was the church authorities who
persecuted Jesus and contrived His death!
Immediately we follow Jesus, both the natural world
and Satanic forces will rise up against us.

Paul also faced severe suffering and martyrdom. All
the disciples except John were also martyred. Can we
expect anything less costly? Jesus taught us about the
cost of discipleship and warned us to count that cost
before deciding to follow Him. We should not be
surprised when we face opposition and hardship but
recognise that we are caught up in a battle between
good and evil.

However, the good news is that this is a battle like no

other. All through history, battles have been fought and millions have been killed in conflict. But in none of these battles was the outcome known beforehand. In direct contrast, we know the final outcome of the battle in which we fight. We know with absolute certainty that God is sovereign and that no power can defeat Him. As Paul writes, if God is for us, who can succeed in standing against us?

We need to broaden our outlook. Death is not the end for those of us who trust in Christ. This life is just a brief time of preparation and testing before an eternal adventure when:

> *He will wipe away every tear from their eyes; and there will no longer be any death; there will no longer be any mourning, or crying, or pain;* (Revelation 21:4a)

Our death is only the end of a brief beginning. We may be martyred, but that will not be the end for us. There is no power who can rob us of our eternal destiny. If God prepared the Garden of Eden, providing everything for Adam and Eve's needs and enjoyment, how much more has He prepared a wonderful future for us to enjoy forever.

Day 99

The Fewest of all Peoples

The Lord did not set His love on you nor
choose you because you were more in
number than any of the peoples, for you
were the fewest of all peoples.
Deuteronomy 7:7

We need to clear our mind completely from any thoughts that God chose us because we were in any way better than other people. God does not choose us because He finds any merit in us, whether it is in our appearance, or education, or stature, or parentage. God does not need our talents, status, training, or experience. God chooses those who will allow Him to work in them and through them. God is looking for people who will submit to His lordship, listen to His voice and obey Him, for those who are prepared to take risks and to step out in faith, for those who are humble and see their need to depend on Him.

This may not sound like good news, but in reality it is exceedingly good news for this reason: none of us need to be eliminated, for the qualities needed are possible for every one of us. None of us need to be barred for reasons that we cannot change. Even those of us who have committed heinous crimes or those of us with severe physical or mental disabilities are not exempt. There is no one who has fallen too far for God's arms to reach down and to lift them up:

> *He brought me up out of the pit of destruction, out of the miry clay, And He set my feet upon a rock making my footsteps firm.* Psalm 40:2

God chose the Israelites because they were the fewest in number and would not therefore be able to overcome their many enemies in their own strength. Their limited number would require them to trust in God and not in themselves. Remember how God reduced Gideon's army before giving them an amazing victory.

We need to come to the essential understanding that God does not need our good ideas or physical strength, and that we cannot bear spiritual fruit with worldly ideas and methods. Spiritual fruit can only be achieved through the power of the Holy Spirit within us. In direct contrast, when we trust in our own very limited resources, strength, and abilities, we deny ourselves God's unlimited provision and miraculous power.

Day 100

The Supremacy of Love

The one who does not love does not know
God, for God is love... God is love, and the
one who abides in love abides in God, and
God abides in him. 1 John 4:8,16b

We have considered the supreme importance of love in many previous studies. These two verses from John's letter emphasise that it is an essential aspect of the gospel. John tells us emphatically that if we do not love we do not know God. If we want to evaluate our maturity as a Christian believer, perhaps there is no better test than this one: the more we demonstrate love to those around us, both friends and enemies, the closer we are to God.

Let us ask ourselves why this is true. Paul tells us in his letter to the church in Rome that God pours His love into our hearts. It is therefore true that if we remain close to Him, our hearts will be filled to overflowing with His love and it will pour out onto those around us.

For a practical example: if you hold a glass under a running tap, it will only take a few moments before the water overflows onto the whole area around it. However, if you move the glass just a few inches to one side of the tap, the glass will remain dry and empty.

In contrast to God's love, our love is conditional. We love, hoping to receive some benefit in return. It may be a genuine need for companionship and self-worth, but it leads to a tendency to love those who can give us something in return. We find it difficult to love the unlovely, and especially those who abuse us. It is when we are filled with God's unconditional love, that we are enabled to love those who can give us nothing in return.

Many years ago, I read the testimony of a man who died briefly while he was in hospital. I cannot remember all the details of his near-death experience. There was one point, however, which I shall never forget. When he met with Jesus and his whole life flashed before him, Jesus asked him what he had done with this life. His reply included his various achievements including exam results and positions held. To which Jesus replied: none of these matter at all. The only thing which matters is now much you have loved people.

Faith in Action

Working in Partnership with Churches in Africa

Faith in Action is a Christian Charity which was registered with the Charity Commission in the UK in 1984. We have worked with over twelve churches in Tanzania, Uganda, Burundi, Malawi, Zambia, and Mozambique, but have more recently focused on a close partnership with a church based in Blantyre, Malawi. Most of their churches are in the Lower Shire, the poorest area in the south of this country which is separated by a thousand-metre escarpment.

Our ministry includes the production and provision of Christian resources including the printing of over 100,000 Bible studies in Chichewa, the setting up of a large variety of development and health-care projects including solar irrigation schemes, the provision of funds for a micro business loan scheme, and a ministry into prisons and to the 350 people who live and work in a rubbish dump on the outskirts of Blantyre, where they scavenge for items to sell and are often reduced to eating mouldy food which they find in the rubbish.

We believe that this is where the focus of the church should be: with people who are isolated from, and rejected by, the world around them, demonstrating to them the wonderful love, mercy and graciousness of God, and helping them to turn their lives around permanently.

Address

14 Gabriel Road, Maidenbower, Crawley, RH10 7LG

Telephone: 01293 886596

Website: www.faithinaction.uk.com

Email: sally@faithinaction.uk.com

Registered Charity No: 293961

(blank)